HOW TO SAY

AND

KEEP YOUR FRIENDS

Peer Pressure Reversal for Teens and Preteens

Second Edition

Sharon Scott, L.P.C., L.M.F.T.

Illustrated by
Rick Murnane

Human Resource Development Press, Inc.
Amherst   Massachusetts

Published by Human Resource Development Press, Inc.
22 Amherst Road
Amherst, Massachusetts 01002
800-822-2801 (U.S. and Canada)
413-253-3488
413-253-3490 (fax)
http://www.hrdpress.com

First Edition, First Printing, June 1986
Second Edition, First Printing, July 1997

Printed in the United States of America

ISBN 0-87425-409-4

Typesetting by Michele Anctil

Cover Design by Eileen Klockars

Editorial work by Mary George

Dedicated with love . . .

to the memory of Arlene McKinnon,
a great friend and traveling buddy,
and
to fourteen very special kids

Other Books by Sharon Scott

Peer Pressure Reversal: An Adult Guide to Developing a Responsible Child, 2nd Edition

Positive Peer Groups

When to Say Yes! and Make More Friends

Too Smart for Trouble

Not Better . . . Not Worse . . . Just Different

Too Cool for Drugs (with Dr. Wayne Hindmarsh)

Life's Not Always Fair: A Child's Guide to Managing Emotions

TABLE OF CONTENTS

PREFACE.. ix

1. INTRODUCTION   1

2. STORIES OF NEGATIVE PEER PRESSURE ..   13

3. LEARNING PEER PRESSURE REVERSAL   31

    Step 1:   Check Out the Scene....................   40

    Step 2:   Make a Good Decision   49

    Step 3:   Act to Avoid Trouble....................   58

4. PPR IN ACTION   93

5. TOBACCO, ALCOHOL, OTHER
    DRUGS, SEX, AND VIOLENCE................. 107

6. SUMMARY: THEY CHOOSE, YOU LOSE....... 157

ABOUT THE AUTHOR 161

PREFACE

When I was growing up in Denison, Texas, I had peer pressure decisions to make just like you do. And I, too, worried at times whether my friends would like me if I didn't go along with some of their dumb or wrong ideas. Then somehow it dawned on me that *true* friends liked me for being me—they liked my corny sense of humor, my loyalty, my honesty, my friendliness. The realization led to an important personal decision: that I wanted to do *my own* thinking and that I really didn't care what others were doing. To this day, I remain fiercely independent. As far as I know, I've never lost a friend because I didn't go along with a trouble-making idea.

There is a big difference, however, between your growing-up years and mine. You're growing up much faster and are called upon to make some really tough decisions when still fairly young. For instance, I wasn't even offered alcohol by friends until I was 18 years old and in college; today in our nation, the average age for being offered alcohol is about 12 years old!

Clearly, to get by in this fast-paced world, you and your peers will need more skills than any previous generation of youth. My goal is to give you some assistance, to help you when you say no to a friend and want to do it in such a way that you remain buddies. This goal also includes preparing you for some tough choices you will have to make in the future, so that you will be ready to handle those choices when the time comes.

I wish to acknowledge several individuals who have assisted me along the way, whose contributions to my education, career, and growth made this book possible. My gratitude extends to Dr. Robert Carkhuff, Dr. Tom Collingwood, Dr. Bernard Berenson, and Dr. Richard Pierce for helping me develop a strong skills base. I am also indebted to retired Lt. R.D. Wilson, who developed the Dallas Police Department's groundbreaking First Offender Program, where I began formulating Peer Pressure Reversal skills. I also want to thank my private counseling clients who encouraged me to write my first book—a dream I hadn't even thought of!

And thanks also to those kids who've used Peer Pressure Reversal and are standing up for what they believe in.

Sharon Scott

1.

INTRODUCTION

- *Houston, Texas. A 17-year-old boy kills his best friend and another boy during a drag race when he loses control of his car and veers into the crowd of onlookers.*

- *St. Louis, Missouri. The quarterback of a high school football team is benched by the coach because of his use of marijuana, causing his team to lose the state championship.*

- *Winter Haven, Florida. A 14-year-old girl has just learned that she is pregnant and is confused and depressed about what to do.*

- *Amherst, Massachusetts. An 18-year-old girl flunks out of college because of partying and skipping classes.*

- *Austin, Texas. A 17-year-old boy dies of acute alcoholic poisoning while playing drinking games at a fraternity party; his cold body is found slumped in a corner at 3 A.M.; his "friends" say they thought he had just passed out.*

- *Walla Walla, Washington. A 13-year-old girl is arrested with her friends for shoplifting jewelry. Now that she has a police record, her career goal of being an attorney may have to be changed.*

What do these true scenarios have in common? Peer pressure. In each example, someone had a friend encouraging him or her to engage in harmful or illegal activity. The persons applying the peer pressure certainly did not want their friends to get hurt or die. I'm sure they just wanted to be cool and have some fun. However, when we make poor choices the consequences can be serious—even deadly.

This book is about decisions and about courage—**your** decisions and **your** courage to do what is right.

When you were a toddler, your parents made all of your decisions for you. As you entered elementary school, you probably began making some simple decisions about your choice of clothes and activities. Now that you are in your teens, you have lots of decisions to make: whom to choose for friends, what study habits to develop, how to spend your weekends, what classes to take, whether to get a part-time job, and so forth. You want to make these choices on your own. However, you must get that privilege from your parents, who will be thinking about whether or not you can make **good** decisions. They will base how much freedom to give you on your history of making either good choices or lousy ones. If you've made good choices up to now, this book will help you keep up the fine work; if you've made lousy ones, this book will help you begin **now** to make good ones!

Your reward for being able to think wisely on your own is more freedom, less nagging, fewer reminders, and more privileges. The world of adults works this way also—those who make good choices get more money, promotions, and privileges at work. So you are actually improving a skill that you will need all of your life: how to make good decisions for yourself and not let others interfere with your choices.

The goal of *How to Say No and Keep Your Friends* is to help you with the toughest of all decisions: peer pressure decisions. What exactly is peer pressure? *Webster's Dictionary* defines a peer as "a person of the same rank or ability." More commonly, we think of a peer as someone who is close to our age. And pressure is when they verbally, not physically, encourage us to think as they think, act as they act, or do as they do.

Peer pressure can be positive or negative. Positive peer pressure is when others encourage us to study hard, play our best, try out for a team, ask someone out, or join an activity. Positive peer pressure is also when someone talks another out of doing something wrong. Your school may have a program in peer helping. That is another example of positive peer pressure because it involves people encouraging others to be their best. Positive peer pressure is great as it sometimes is the "push" we need to try something new.

Negative peer pressure, the focus of this book, is when a person close to our age encourages us *with words* to do something that is either wrong, dangerous, harmful, or illegal. You may be thinking, "Nobody makes me do anything wrong!" And, unless you are involved in an armed robbery someday, you are correct! No one *makes* us do something that we shouldn't do; however, they often beg, bribe, or tease us to do things we shouldn't. Others may even make fun of us or put us down if we don't go along with their idea.

Negative peer pressure may sound like some of these "famous" lines:

"Come on, it'll be fun. We won't get caught."

"It's no big deal. Everybody is doing it."

"I thought you were my friend. If you were, you'd do this with me."

"Trust me. No one will find out."

"Be cool."

"Don't act like a nerd."

"I dare you to do this."

"If you really loved me, you'd do this."

"What a goody-goody! You're no fun."

"Grow up."

"I'll give you _____ if you'll do this for me."

"If you don't do this with me, I'm not going to invite you to my party."

"Are you chicken?"

"Mama's baby!"

We've all heard these lines. They can easily get us into trouble if we don't know how to quickly handle them!

It's also important to recognize that sometimes peer pressure is nonverbal. It's expressed in the way friends look at us like we're stupid or something. Or sometimes we *think* others are looking at us funny (whether or not they really are!). These "looks" can also encourage us to do what others want us to do.

It's important to handle peer pressure lines (or "looks") in such a way that we still keep our friends—as well as our dignity.

Most of the time when we make poor decisions it's because we're listening to others and just not thinking. Rarely do we do things that are wrong all by ourselves. I became aware of the intensity of negative peer pressure years ago when I worked for the Dallas Police Department, as Director of the First Offender Program there. My staff of counselors and I worked with thousands of young people between the ages of 10 and 16 who had made such poor decisions that they had actually broken a law and been taken into custody (arrested).

What kind of kids do you think would break laws and get busted? Usually people answer that they were probably mean, tough kids who didn't know right from wrong. Other common answers include that their parents, if they had any around, didn't care about them; they were probably poor, belonged to gangs, wore punk clothing, and had bad attitudes.

Well, the truth is that some did have bad attitudes and some were poor, but just as many were from wealthy families. The majority of the arrested kids had parents who did care. And these kids **did** know right from wrong! Many of them were active in sports, cheerleading, religious youth groups, Scouts, music lessons, and so forth. Most were normal, nice kids who knew better.

Why then did they break the law? When asked, they usually gave one of these three answers: "I didn't know what to say to my friends! And everybody else was doing it."; "They told me it was no big deal. I didn't think we would get caught."; or "They were calling me names. What would you have done?"

While in the "holding room" as their parents were being contacted and the police were deciding what action to take, these kids would be scared, frequently crying and arguing with their friends over whose idea it had been to cause trouble. They would now try to blame each other for the poor decision they'd made! And it didn't really matter whose idea it had been. They had *all* broken the law and *each* would pay the consequences for his or her actions. The old saying is true: If you can't do the time, don't do the crime!

Crimes committed by teens and preteens have risen drastically over the years. Our society has become more violent. Drive-by shootings and gang activity are common in many neighborhoods. Stores where we shop have to raise prices because there is so much shoplifting. Alcohol and other drugs are harming and killing many youth. Unhappiness, depression, and suicide have increased. The United States has the highest rate of teen pregnancy of any industrialized country. These serious problems all begin when one person says to a buddy, "Hey, I've got a great idea, and we won't get caught."

I've asked thousands of teens who attend my work-shops what group of peers it's hardest to say no to. And they always answer that it can be especially difficult to say no to best friends, older kids, popular youth, and boyfriends or girlfriends. And the first years of middle school, high school, and college can be particularly tough because we want to impress the upper classmen. In our efforts to be "Joe" or "Josephine Cool," we often do dumb things to show off for older students.

Why is it hard to say no to these people? Basically, we're afraid that if we don't go along with their ideas, they won't like us and may even drop us as a friend. In other words, we're afraid of rejection by people whom we really want to impress.

Let's examine this concept a little closer. If a friend drops you because you won't do whatever he or she wants to do, what kind of friend is that person? Most people would say a lousy one. Such "friends" want to be the boss or leader. The friendship is therefore based on them controlling us. Not the kind of friendships that most of us would really want!

So what really happens when we turn down a dumb idea of a *true* friend? Some may tease us. Others may get mad, and some may even call us a name. The big question then is how long will a good friend stay mad when you don't go along with the bad idea? The most common answer I hear is a few hours to one day! Well, big deal! I think most of us can live with that! If you don't learn to live with a bit of rejection, then others will be in control of your decisions the rest of your life!

In fact, sometimes when we don't go along with a friend's bad idea, he or she won't act alone on it. So we may have even helped our friend!

We may also fear that if we don't go along with bad ideas, our friends will talk about us behind our backs. Two centuries ago, Benjamin Franklin noted that "He who gossips to you, will gossip of you." Meaning that gossips gossip! If you do something right, they'll call you a goody-goody or nerd. If you do something wrong, they'll say you're easy or stupid. You can't win with a gossip, because they'll gossip no matter what you do. We certainly don't need to live our lives based on what people may or may not be saying about us.

In Chapter 2, we'll look at true stories about nice kids like you who made some poor decisions involving negative peer pressure, and we'll see what the results were.

Chapter 3 will teach you the Peer Pressure Reversal skills that I've taught to over one million people. Most kids use the skills within 24 hours of learning them. Why so fast? Research shows that 87 percent of teens face at least one negative peer pressure situation every day! It could be pressure to skip school, cheat on a test, fight, gossip, shoplift, sneak out, drink alcohol, cut someone out of your group, lie to parents about a destination, drive too fast, break curfew, smoke a cigarette, loan homework answers, have a party without permission, haze younger students, harass a substitute teacher, smoke marijuana, trespass on private property, have friends over when no parent is at home, forge a parent's signature on a school paper, sneak in an R-rated movie, make a prank phone call, and so forth. Peer Pressure Reversal (or PPR for short) is simply a method for how to say no and be able to keep your friends (and your dignity) as well.

Chapter 4 involves practicing what we've learned. We can test our abilities to think and react quickly. Have we got the smarts and the guts to use what we've learned?

And, finally, Chapter 5 will focus on several peer pressure situations which are so serious that should we become involved in them, it could be life-threatening.

I truly believe that all of us—old or young—must take responsibility for our actions. We must choose to do good things and be kind to others, and in this process we may just make this world a safer, fun place for us all to live.

2.

STORIES OF

NEGATIVE

PEER PRESSURE

Few people realize that negative peer pressure begins when we're about three years old. You may recall from years ago a little friend saying to you, "If you don't play this game with me, then you can just go home." That's a perfect example of "little kid" peer pressure. When we heard our friend say that to us, some of us probably cried because our feelings were hurt. Others of us probably grabbed the game away from the kid and bopped him or her over the head with it! Of course, neither "method" is a tactful way to handle peer pressure! As we get older, the peer pressure invitations become more serious, as we'll see in the following stories.

The following are *true* examples of teens like you who had some difficulty handling negative peer pressure (only their names and minor details have been changed, to protect their privacy). Most of these youth I know personally, as they were clients of mine in my counseling practice. A few came to my attention through newspaper articles. The situations in their stories aren't at all unusual—kids around the world find themselves in such situations all the time. They will remind us of how tough negative peer pressure can be.

☆ Star Football Player ☆

I'll call him Tad. He was a star football player at his school. He had shown tremendous natural ability since he began playing football in fifth grade. Tad was a B student and had quite a few friends. He was not, however, a member of the "in" crowd, one of the really popular students. As a freshman he had not been invited to many parties. Now in the tenth grade, he was excited to be getting quite a few invitations to attend after-game parties.

He was surprised to find that most of these parties revolved around drinking alcohol—mainly beer and wine coolers. When he was first offered a beer, he turned it down with the excuse that he was on the team and needed to stay in good shape. No one tried to *make* him drink alcohol—that's not cool. All his friends did was offer.

As he attended more parties, he began to doubt himself. He figured that he wouldn't continue to be invited to the parties if he didn't drink with his friends. So he started to have "just one." After a while it became "I can handle two." After a couple of months, he was chugging quite a few beers with these kids. Then he decided to try pot. His usage of both alcohol and pot increased to usage during the week too.

Soon he was missing an occasional football practice, was often late to his first-period class, and wasn't playing as well because his body wasn't functioning as well. His parents talked to him, as did his coach. They weren't sure what the problem was, although they all suspected it was use of chemicals. He got benched and became seriously depressed. His parents brought him to me for counseling.

After many soul-searching sessions, including learning the Peer Pressure Reversal skills, he figured out that he didn't have to use alcohol or other drugs in order to have fun or to keep friends. His self-esteem soared as he learned that true friends like you for who you really are— not for some "fake" person hopped up on chemicals.

By the time he reached his junior year, he had college scouts looking at him because he had been selected the best cornerback in his region!

♪ The After-School Blues ♪

I'll call her Erika. She was new to town and anxious to make new friends in her seventh-grade class. Her parents both worked and had instructed her to do her homework and chores after she walked home from school. She was not allowed to have friends over until her parents came home.

One day some of her friends dropped by to see her soon after she arrived home. She thought it would be okay to stand on her porch and talk to them. They wanted to come inside, but she explained her parents' rule: no friends in the house unless her parents were home.

The following week, the same group returned, this time with a plan that Erika did not know about. They insisted that she let them come in for just a minute to use the bathroom. Erika didn't feel quite as strong turning them down again, so she said they could come in for just a minute. She was shocked to find that only one kid went to the bathroom; the rest went into the kitchen, pulled out some liquor they had brought, and mixed it with soft drinks from her refrigerator. Not wanting to offend her new friends, she had a drink with them. They stayed quite a while, but left before her parents arrived home.

This became a regular routine. She was having fun and feeling important. However, her parents began fussing at her because her chores weren't done. She was staying up late trying to get her homework done, and this also made her parents upset with her.

Erika's new friends began to encourage her to skip school with them. One day she finally got up the nerve to do it. What a shock when all of them got picked up by the truancy officer and were taken to the police station! Her parents were so disappointed, for Erika had always been a good student. Erika was grounded for two weeks, and during that time everything went along smoothly.

When the grounding period was over, she began letting the friends visit after school again. Her parents knew something was up and came home early from work one day. They caught Erika drinking with her friends. Erika lost almost all of her privileges and was forbidden to associate with those kids again. Her parents called the friends' parents, and the friends were grounded too.

Once again, giving in to peer pressure caused a loss of trust and freedom and forced adults to make decisions for someone who seemed incapable of making good decisions on her own. I met Erika at this point, as her family came to me for counseling. Erika came to realize that her "friends" had been using her—they needed a house with no parents and a willing kid to let them have their parties. They had no use for her after she began following the rule of not having friends over until her parents were home. Erika worked on her self-esteem and began making some quality friends.

✗ The Porsche Puzzle ✗

Jim, age 15, convinced his parents that they could trust him to stay home alone while they attended the out-of-town funeral of a relative. They did not like the idea, but he explained that he needed to stay home to study for final exams. Before his parents left, they reminded him to keep the doors locked, to check in with the neighbors each evening, and not to let any friends come over. They would be gone only two days.

After his parents left, Jim called up some friends to brag about being home alone. The friends' one-word response was "PARTY!" Jim told them a party would be fun, but that he could not have company over. Before he could say another word, his friends replied, "We'll come in through the alley so the neighbors don't see us." Then they hung up.

When they arrived, Jim was not strong-willed enough to stop them from coming in. Studying for finals suddenly seemed very boring. So the party began.

One guy walked into the garage and whistled loudly when he saw the sports car owned by Jim's father—a Porsche. He rushed back into the house and encouraged Jim to drive everyone around in it. Jim declined, saying he didn't yet have a driver's license. His friends persisted, though, and liking all of this attention, Jim finally agreed to drive them around as soon as it got dark.

You can guess what happened. While showing off for his friends, Jim took a corner too fast and wrecked his dad's car. It was in a ditch and they couldn't get it out! Everyone had an idea of what to do; Jim thought the best one was to act like the car had been stolen and wrecked by a car thief. So Jim and his friends bashed in the windshield and then damaged Jim's garage door to make it appear that someone had broken in. Jim put the car keys back where he had found them, and his friends went home.

Jim called his parents and told them someone had stolen the car. His father flew home early and called the police as soon as he arrived. The police investigated and, after tracking down several leads, concluded that Jim had done it. His father could not believe what he was hearing.

I had met Jim a week before this happened, in a counseling session with him and his parents. They had been frustrated by some poor decisions on Jim's part, including skipping school, drinking, and cheating. Now in need of further help, Jim's father called me, and I agreed with the police that his son had done this and was lying to him. I suggested that he continue to talk to Jim.

He did. Finally, at 3 A.M., Jim tearfully admitted to his father that he indeed had wrecked the Porsche and tried to make it look like the car had been stolen. Jim's parents were so angry with him, and so frightened by his inability to make good choices, that they decided to send him away to a very strict military school. Further counseling, they felt, was just not strong enough a measure to get Jim's attention.

I never saw Jim again, but I hope that he finally matured and learned that real friends don't keep encouraging you to do things that are wrong. I also hope that he came to see himself as the neat person he truly was—a person who didn't have to show off to make friends and keep them.

⊕ **In the Dark of the Night** ⊕

Fourteen-year-old Jacque's good friend, Angela, was visiting overnight. They had watched a movie, had shared a pizza, and now were calling friends to see what they were doing. One of the guys they called offered to come by and drive them to get a soft drink. J.D. was 16 and old enough to drive. They were really impressed, but told him they were not allowed to date yet. He laughed and said, "It's not a date. We'll have something to drink and then I'll take you back home." Angela was really excited and tried to convince Jacque to go. Jacque explained that her mother would never allow this.

After much discussion, they agreed to sneak out at midnight to go for a quick ride with J.D. To their surprise, when he arrived he had another guy with him. Instead of taking them to get a soft drink, J.D. drove straight to a dark area of a park. He and Angela got out of the car and, giggling, walked away.

Without saying a word, the guy in the car with Jacque began to take her clothes off. She was so scared that she said nothing as he molested her. She was hurt and humiliated. The others returned to the car and J.D. drove them home.

Jacque's mother found her crying the next day and learned of what happened the previous evening. Jacque was embarrassed because the guys had told practically the whole school about it. Jacque's mother wanted to call the police, but Jacque was afraid of even more publicity. And Jacque was scared that she might be pregnant. Her mother scheduled her for a doctor's appointment and for a counseling appointment with me. I begin to help her understand how she had let others, Angela and both guys, control her. She knew for sure that she needed to learn how to say no and stand up for herself. She knew also that she would never again sneak out with guys.

The good news from the doctor: she was not pregnant. The bad news: she had gotten genital warts from the molester. And she would have to take an AIDS test in six months to make sure that he had not given her that deadly disease.

➥ The Getaway ➥

Lyle was an all-American boy during his years in middle school—along with having good grades, good looks, and lots of friends, he was a star athlete in football. The summer after he graduated from middle school, though, his family moved to a new town. Lyle was nervous about starting high school there. He worried about making new friends, whether he would make the freshman team, and so forth.

When school began he picked some of the senior guys to hang out with. Lyle was big for his age and fit right in with them. Lyle made the football team. His new friends congratulated him, but commented that football was a lot of hard work for nothing.

Lyle soon found out that his new friends ran in the "fast lane"—skipping school, drinking alcohol, smoking marijuana, and juggling lots of girlfriends, each of whom were told that she was the one and only. Lyle did not get involved in this trouble with them because he had been taught better, plus he could use the excuse that he had to keep in shape for football. But as time went by, he wondered if they thought of him as a wimp since he didn't drink with them or do other drugs.

So that he didn't feel left out, he had a beer with them one night when they were cruising around. Another day he cut a class with them. These actions seemed innocent enough, so he accepted more trouble invitations from them, including smoking pot. It wasn't but a few months before his grades dropped, his football career sunk, and his parents were on his back about his behavior, also complaining that he dressed "too tough-looking." He told his parents to lay off, that he would live his life the way he wanted to.

Several weeks before Christmas, he and three of these older friends were driving around drinking and drugging. They were complaining about having no money to buy their girlfriends presents for the holidays. The driver of the car said, "I've got a great idea! Let's rob a convenience store and split the money." They all laughed and drank some more as they thought about this big joke.

At 1 A.M. the very stoned driver pulled up in front of a convenience store and announced, "This is it. No one's around. We can pull this off easy!" His friends were stunned and said they thought he had been joking. He told them they were cowards if they didn't help him. Not thinking clearly or wanting to be called names, they agreed to help. He told two of the guys to stay in the car and be lookouts. He told Lyle to come in the store with him.

Never having committed a robbery before, they didn't know what to do. At first, they played the video games. Then the driver went over to the clerk and told him to hand over all the money from the cash register. The clerk reached for a gun that he kept under the counter. When he did, the driver pulled a gun out of his coat pocket and shot the clerk at close range. Blood gushed from the clerk's chest.

The driver rushed from the store, jumped into his car, and sped away. Leaving *guess who?* inside. Lyle stood in the store in shock. Then he began running, and ran two miles until he got home, dove into bed, and covered up.

In the meantime, the clerk was found and rushed to the hospital. He was barely alive. As the police investigated they got a description of Lyle, who had been seen running from the scene. When the police went to Lyle's home to talk with him, he became hysterical.

The end of this story is that all four boys were arrested. Charges included attempted murder (the clerk lived but would have disabilities the rest of his life), possession of narcotics, armed robbery, and minors in possession of alcohol. All four of these boys suffered severe consequences, including a lengthy prison term for the 17-year-old (who was an adult under Texas law). Lyle's parents brought him to me following his lockup in juvenile detention. He was so depressed about the poor choices that he had made that he was considering suicide. Here again we have a good kid who made bad decisions because of listening to friends. Lyle had been raised right and he knew better. Lyle eventually got himself back to the "old" (and better) Lyle. He began going to religious youth-group meetings, became highly selective of friends, got his GED, and then enrolled in college.

✏ Newspaper Accounts of Peer Pressure ✏

☞ *From Ohio:* Two girls, ages 12 and 13, devised a plot to kill a teacher who had scolded them for not paying attention. Their classmates found out about it and bet $200 on the outcome—a response that, according to the two girls, put them on the spot and made them feel they had to carry out their plan. Both girls ended up in juvenile detention prior to the actual attempt on the teacher's life.

☞ *From New Jersey:* Five students, ages 17 and 18, who were sports stars from an affluent school, lured a mentally retarded 17-year-old girl from a city park to one of their homes. There they raped her while other guys looked on. They were arrested and charged with aggravated sexual assault.

☞ *From Texas:* Eight teenaged guys trespassed onto private property in a rural area outside of town to have a post-midnight party. There were some large tanks on the land and five of the guys decided to climb on them. One kicked in a tank's hatch to find out what was inside. He lit a match to see better. The match ignited fumes in the tank, which was partially full of crude oil, and set off a massive explosion with flames leaping 15 feet into the air. The guys who had remained on the ground rushed the friends who had been thrown off the tank to the hospital. They were in critical condition with extensive burns. One of the guys was missing and was not found until the next day. His body had been thrown by the explosion 100 yards into a wooded area.

☞ *From Pennsylvania:* Four teenagers were cruising around in a pickup truck after a beer-drinking party. Their truck collided with a telephone pole, and one boy was thrown out onto the road. His friends picked him up and dragged him across a field to the edge of a thick woods. They were afraid of getting into trouble for drinking so they left their friend and did not go for help. The injured boy died.

☞ *From Texas:* Four teenagers took a shortcut through a church parking lot and almost drove over a girl lying on the ground covered in blood. They thought she was dead, but were unsure. Shocked and frightened, it took them *40 minutes* of discussion before they called the police. It is uncertain whether a quicker decision to call for help would have saved the girl's life. The girl, who had been voted "Most Beautiful" at her school, was dead on arrival at the hospital. Who killed her, or why, is still unknown. Her car had broken down and she was walking the four blocks back to her home for help when someone killed her.

☞ *From Oklahoma:* A 17-year-old boy died and his buddy suffered a brain seizure and severe retardation after drinking "moonshine" they'd been dared to try. The boy offering the alcohol was actually giving his friends drinks of methanol, a fuel additive properly used by his father, who was a professional racecar driver.

Does *Anyone* Have the Smarts and the Guts to Manage Negative Peer Pressure?

"If stupidity were a crime, you would all deserve life without parole," said Judge Joe Kendall to 12 young men, ages 17 to 19, at their sentencing hearing. All of these guys had played high school football together (three had played on the winning state-championship team together) and several had already accepted athletic scholarships to major universities where they planned to begin classes in a few weeks. These were good kids who had no previous criminal records.

In order to have extra money for gold jewelry, tuxedos, and limos for prom night—and to "get attention," as many said—they had been involved in a string of armed robberies of fast-food restaurants and video stores. The crimes were inside jobs as, in most cases, one of the robbers worked at the location that they hit and allowed his friends to put guns in the faces of co-workers! They boasted to their friends about the "easy" money, and more and more joined in.

Judge Kendall sentenced 10 of the young men to prison terms ranging from two to 25 years. Of the remaining two, one got 75 days in boot camp and the other got 10 years' probation. Most were remorseful, embarrassed for what they had put their families through, and apologetic. One said he was so distressed by his actions that he had considered suicide but then decided it would just make a bad situation worse. None of those things helped in a court of law, however. It was too late. One boy said, "I was not strong enough to say no when the guys were talking about doing these things that I knew were wrong." Each agreed that peer pressure had influenced his actions. That may be the reason, but it's no excuse.

Let me tell you, however, about a thirteenth guy who did not embarrass himself or his parents, did not have to cry about his actions, and went off to college on a basketball scholarship rather than to the penitentiary with his friends. The *Dallas Times Herald* reported that Sean Townsend had been asked twice by his close friends to join in on the robberies. It was their senior year and they were planning lavish parties and good times.

Sean said, "I was kind of tempted to go," as the new clothes and jewelry he saw on his friends were impressive. He was told that he could just drive, but after sleeping on the invitation, he decided that he could do without the finery. He added, "I couldn't see myself doing something like that. I thought even if I drive, I'm an accessory to the crime. My parents would have been hurt." So he told his friends no and began edging away from them, concentrating on his schoolwork and college plans. The last big blast with his friends came on prom night. The others wore costly gold rings and chains that he knew had been bought with stolen money. According to the newspaper, Sean wore jewelry borrowed from his father.

In an effort to be supportive of his friends, Sean went to the courthouse during one of the hearings. He had to run from the courtroom with watery eyes until he could gain his composure, as he couldn't stand to see his friends in the situation they were in.

Sean is a really good kid—just like the other guys. There is one difference, however: he had the smarts and the guts to make a good decision, to think on his own, and to know that you don't have to do anything to impress *real* friends. Real friends like you for who you really are—even without gold jewelry, fancy clothes, and fine cars. Congratulations, Sean, and have a good life!

3.

LEARNING

PEER

PRESSURE

REVERSAL

When you are faced with a negative peer pressure invitation, how do you currently handle it? Most people answer that they say no or walk away, or sometimes, not knowing what to say, they go along with the dumb or trouble idea. Saying no and walking away can be effective, but many people say they are uncomfortable using those techniques. If they just say no, the friend often keeps on them and then they feel stuck! And, they say, just walking away can appear rude. At times, that may be necessary; at other times, it may be inappropriate. And giving in to the negative peer pressure can get a person in a lot of trouble, so that's not good either.

What kind of trouble can you get into? Well, it depends on what the situation is, where you are, how strict your parents are, possibly your age, and what kind of person you really want to be! Sometimes trouble just leads to getting fussed at and being disappointed in yourself. Other times trouble can lead to a visit with the principal, being suspended or sent to a different school, or even being expelled. Some trouble can lead to detention hall, a police record, or even lockup. And the most serious trouble can cost someone his or her life, including your own. There-fore, it's important to learn *how* to say no in such a way that you'll use it when you need to. And you'll know that you can still be liked and have friends at the same time.

As you continue to think about how you currently manage any negative peer pressure that comes your way, see if you fit any of the characteristics of Sylvia Snob or Walter Wimp. Or maybe at times you act like a Chuck Cool. What I hope you are—or become by reading this book—is a Chris Confident. Read on for the way they each handle trouble in this fictional story.

☆ Let's Party! ☆

Kevin is throwing a big bash at his house Friday night after the football game. Most kids think it's going to be the usual pizza and soft drinks and home by midnight. Everyone is surprised by the actual situation: Kevin's parents aren't there, the house is crowded with almost more people than it can hold, and alcohol is readily available. Let's peep in and see how several teens handle this very common situation.

Sylvia is one of the first to arrive. Sylvia, a good student, is shocked by what she finds at the party. She is barely past the front door when she loudly announces, "I can't believe you all would stay at a party like this! I'm certainly not going to hang out with alcoholics! Goodbye." She slams the door on her way out.

Walter is one of the next to arrive. He's surprised by the wild party, but stays anyway. He knows he should leave, but can't think fast enough to figure out just how to do it in a cool way. He sits in a corner to gather his thoughts. Jason comes by and offers him a beer. "Hey, big Walter, how about a cold one?"

Walter, in a soft voice, replies, "I've never had a beer and don't think I should start now."

"Aw, then it's time to try it. Just one. You're not gonna get drunk." He hands Walter the beer. Walter sips on the beer and frowns. He hates the taste of it, but keeps drinking because all the other kids seem to be drinking.

Chuck, the star baseball player, hits the party with a bang. Everyone likes Chuck. And no one talks Chuck into trouble. He's perceived as being strong. What they don't know is that Chuck can talk *himself* into trouble. He feels he has a reputation to live up to. He's actually unsure whether people like him for himself or because he helps win the state championship for the school. He sees the beer and goes to get one. Chuck doesn't like the taste of beer and hates the hangover he has after drinking. Only he knows what happened to him a month ago—that after drinking with some friends, he wrecked his car when he fell asleep at the wheel and hit a tree. He also knows that his coach would bench him if he knew his star player was drinking, as Chuck's always sluggish after he drinks. But Chuck wants so badly to keep fitting in that he does whatever the crowd is doing.

Looking at the techniques used so far, we can find many weaknesses. Sylvia would be considered a snob because of the way she said no to the trouble. And Walter is plainly wimpy. He can't stand up for himself. And poor Chuck, he's just too cool for his own good.

So how could this situation be handled in a way to save face as well as keep friends?

Chris may have some good techniques. Back to the party . . .

When Chris arrives at the party, she notices that the person answering the door appears to have been drinking. She could leave now, but decides to check out the scene further. When she enters the living room, she notices that the lights are low, no adults are present, and some kids sitting on the sofa appear to be sharing a joint. She quickly decides that this party is not for her. She doesn't want to risk the trouble. She knows there will be many other O.K. parties and activities with her friends in the future.

So Chris quickly waves to a few friends and finds the host, Kevin. She tells him, "I have other plans and can't stay. But I wanted to stop by and say hi. Thanks for asking me, though."

Kevin asks, "Do you think the party is too wild? Is that why you're leaving?"

Chris answers truthfully, "Yeah, I really think it's out of control. You know my parents, they'd kill me if they found out I stayed here, even if I didn't drink or smoke dope."

"Yeah, I know," Kevin says. "And I'm really worried, too. I didn't invite all of these people. They just crashed it. It's getting so noisy that I'm afraid the neighbors are going to call the police."

Chris replies, "Yeah, that could happen. I hope it doesn't for your sake. Good luck, Kevin. See you at school on Monday. Bye."

Chris checked out the scene, made a good decision, and acted on it in just seconds. You can, too.

Life's decision-making road might look like this. Every day most young people are faced with negative peer pressure situations. It starts with simple things when we're young and progresses to more serious trouble invitations as we enter middle and high school. Which side of the road are you on now?

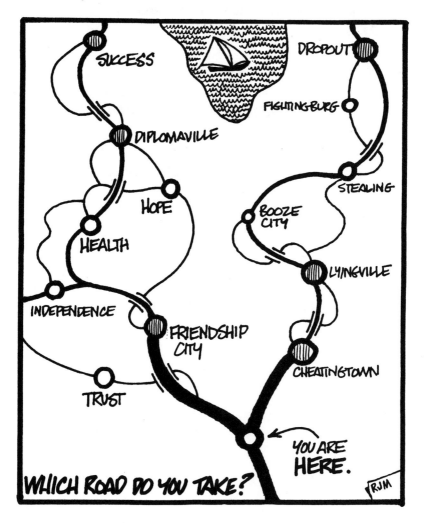

So that you can avoid trouble and take control of your own decisions, let's look at a simple, three-step skill called Peer Pressure Reversal (PPR). I have taught PPR to more than one million people. It has worked for them, and it can work for you, too. I can guarantee you that if you use the steps correctly, they will get you out of tough, trouble situations and let you continue to be liked and have friends.

THE THREE STEPS OF PPR

1. **Check Out the Scene**

2. **Make a Good Decision**

3. **Act to Avoid Trouble**

These steps are not difficult, and they contain plenty of good common sense. Basically, they involve learning how to assess situations quickly, how to think logically and decide what's best for yourself, and how to follow up your decision with appropriate action to protect yourself. You'll be more aware of what's going on around you and therefore be able to use better judgment.

What's in it for you if you use PPR? More privileges! Adults—including parents, teachers, bosses, and coaches—will trust you and know that you make wise choices, and so they will give you more freedom to make your own decisions. For example, professional quarter-backs who can think quickly and logically get to call their own plays; but those who can't assess the situation quickly enough need coaches to send in the plays to them.

I want *you* to be the one who can be trusted to call the plays—the one who knows right from wrong and makes personal decisions based on what is right.

PPR STEP 1:
CHECK OUT THE SCENE

Check Out the Scene suggests that you open your eyes, ears, and mind to what's going on around you—that you pay attention and notice what's happening. In a way, you need to become a "trouble detective." If you learn to read the cues of others well enough, you may be able to recognize trouble before it actually begins and you're asked to participate. That way you can avoid the trouble situation entirely!

It is important to be on the alert for signs of trouble, because the quicker you can recognize potential or actual trouble, the quicker you can react to it. And you *will* have to think fast when you're confronted by situations like this. If you don't, you'll likely get pulled into the trouble!

Check Out the Scene has two substeps:

(A) Look and Listen

(B) Apply the "Trouble?" Rule

(A) Look and Listen

Stay alert. Scope out the scene. If you get this substep down, you'll be more aware of your surroundings and what your friends are doing. To be more aware of your environment is also important as a safety issue.

Look at your friends (the people with you) and see if there is anything unusual in the way they are grouped or behaving. Are they whispering or huddled in secrecy? Are they acting macho? Are they laughing nervously? Also **look** at your location or the place they want you to go. Is it a dangerous-looking place like a deserted street or school, a dark building, or an empty apartment? Does the set-up suggest trouble, such as a party with no adult supervision? Are there kids around whom you don't know or who are a lot older than you are?

Listen carefully to what others are saying. Listen for any hints or hidden suggestions. Sometimes friends leave out parts of their plan to make the plan sound O.K. to us, so you have to clarify exactly what they want you to do. Also **listen** to their tone of voice—is it secretive? Are they trying to persuade you by bribing you ("I'll give you money if you do this for me")? Are they blackmailing you with their friendship ("If you were really my friend, then you'd do this with me")? Are they calling you names ("What a wimp!") or verbally challenging you ("You're a chicken if you don't do this")? Are they claiming that the *whole* world will be involved ("Everybody does it")? Are they giving you a guarantee that parents, teachers, and police won't punish you ("We won't get caught")? Yeah, sure—famous last words!

All of these kinds of peer pressure lines spell *trouble!*

Apply the **Look and Listen** substep to the following scenes and see if you can detect any clues to potential trouble.

1. Your locker at school is located where two halls meet. You can't see what's going on in the next hall, but you hear a lot of people running. You hear locker doors slamming and someone says, "C'mon, let's get him!"

2. It's dusk and the streetlights are just coming on as you walk home. You see some of your friends at the end of the street. As you cross over to say hi to them, you see and hear the following: laughter, a streetlight going dark, and a glass breaking.

3. A friend, who looks worried, grabs you in the hall at school and then looks up and down the hall to see if anyone is coming. The friend says, "Did you do your math? I know you did because you're so smart in that class . . ."

Yep, there are clues in all these situations that indicate potential trouble. In situation Number 1, it *sounds* as if a fight has broken out. If you were to go into that hall, you could easily get involved just by watching. The *look* and *sound* of situation Number 2 suggest that a law (vandalism) has been broken. And judging from the *look* and *sound* of situation Number 3, you'd better be prepared for the friend's next question: "May I copy your homework?"

A person's failure to **look** and **listen** can lead to a serious, even tragic, outcome. Take the case of three guys who were students at The University of Texas. Over spring break, they decided to go to Mexico to do some sightseeing and shopping. One day after checking out some shops together, they got separated, one leaving to find a bathroom while the other two looked in separate but nearby stores.

One of the guys never returned to the group. Unable to find him, his friends called the police and reported him as a missing person. Many people were questioned. Someone recalled seeing a Mexican male, unknown to the student, motioning him over to a pickup truck. That was the only clue.

The end to this true story is that, after a month-long search, the police found the college student's mutilated body (along with 12 others) in the camp of a gang of drug smugglers. The gang members stupidly thought that these slayings would magically protect them from the law. In 1994, all five of the cult members were sentenced to more than 60 years in prison. Because there is no such thing as early parole in Mexico, these five people will die there.

Perhaps the college student forgot an important lesson that we are all taught in childhood: Don't talk to strangers. Being a big, grown-up guy, he probably didn't think anything could happen to him, and so may have missed these basic clues to trouble: isolation from friends (especially in unfamiliar areas); an appeal from a stranger who would have no reason to need help (and, in this case, who likely didn't even speak English); and a motion from a stranger to approach a vehicle (which increases the possibility of abduction). It's a tragedy that might have been avoided by looking and listening carefully.

(B) Apply the "Trouble?" Rule

Once you have **looked** and **listened**, fully observing what is happening in a situation, continue to **check out the scene** by **applying the "Trouble?" Rule**. You need to ask yourself if the situation—what your peers want you to do or get involved in—fits the definition of trouble. The **"Trouble?" Rule** makes this easy by giving you two questions to ask yourself:

- *Does it break a law?*

- *Will it make an authority angry?*

If the answer to either or both of these questions is "yes," then you are definitely facing a trouble situation.

The first **"Trouble?" Rule** question requires you to think about whether what you are being asked to do breaks a law. Whether you agree with the law or not is unimportant to the consequences you may face, including being handcuffed and taken into custody, fined, put on probation, locked up, embarrassed, and so forth. It's important to have some understanding of the law because not knowing that something is illegal is no defense. Most people know that stealing, driving without a license, drinking alcohol underage, burglary, possessing or using narcotics, carrying weapons, arson, and driving under the influence of alcohol are illegal. However I find that many teens don't know that the following actions also break the law: skipping school, drag racing, vandalism (damaging others' property), and making prank phone calls (I'm not talking about when you joke with a good friend, but rather when you call a person and hang up without talking, call and don't say anything, call and curse or threaten someone, and so forth). Also, fighting in public, cursing, and obscene gestures all break a law called disorderly conduct.

The second **"Trouble?" Rule** question requires you to think about whether what you are being asked to do will make someone who is in authority angry. These are things that don't break laws but would upset someone who is in authority. People in authority include parents, teachers, principals, coaches, store owners, employers, youth-group leaders, and neighbors' parents. If your family is spiritual or religious, you may also think of a "supreme being" as an authority figure. No matter what age we are, there are authority figures in our lives whom we should not anger. The consequences of doing so are almost always unpleasant, such as losing privileges, being fired from a job, being kicked off a team or out of an activity, and being reprimanded. We also risk losing people's trust—and it takes a lot of time and effort to regain lost trust!

There are many things involving peer pressure that can anger an authority figure. For example, coming home late, cheating on a test, lying to your parents about where you're going with a friend, sneaking out of the house, copying homework, and passing notes in class. One universal law of human decency is that we should always treat others the way we want to be treated. This also means that we should never treat others the way we *don't* want to be treated. If you are selfish, unkind, or intentionally rude to others, you violate that law and may anger people in authority; consequently, they may put you on restrictions as well as lose respect for you.

Listed below are five social situations. Would any of them lead you to answer "yes" to the **"Trouble?" Rule** questions?

1. Your mom drops you and two friends off at the movie theater. She says she'll pick you up at the same location in exactly two hours. After she drives away, you realize that you've come to the wrong theater. Neither you nor your friends want to see the movie that's playing there, so the three of you walk four blocks to a coffee house. You arrive back at the theater within the two-hour time frame.

2. You and a friend stop off at a convenience store to buy a soft drink. Your friend pays for the soda, but takes a candy bar. You tell your friend to put it back. Your friend refuses. You leave the store with your friend.

3. You attend a chaperoned party with a group of your friends. There's plenty of pizza, good music, and some dancing. You make it home by curfew.

4. While at school, your friend comes up to you and asks you to put a small sack in your locker. When you ask what it is, your friend says, "You don't want to know. Don't worry, though. You're too nice. No one would search your locker."

5. You are riding around with some friends. The driver is old enough to have a driver's license. After a while, several friends begin to pass around a joint. You don't take it.

Of the five examples, only the third one does not involve trouble. The first situation could get an authority angry because you did not ask permission before you changed your plans, and as a result, you might get grounded. As for situations Number 2 and Number 5, you could get arrested since you were present when a crime was committed and you chose not to leave. The small sack in situation Number 4 is surely some kind of trouble— probably marijuana—which is illegal. If you put it in your locker, it would be in your possession and therefore you would be breaking a law.

In summary, Step 1 of Peer Pressure Reversal, **Check Out the Scene**, allows us to be more aware of what's going on around us and to recognize potential trouble quickly. Why do we want to recognize trouble quickly? Because it gives us time to *think*, which leads us to Step 2, **Make a Good Decision**.

PPR STEP 2:
MAKE A GOOD DECISION

The second PPR step is **Make a Good Decision**. If you've taken Step 1 and found that you're being asked to do something that meets the definition of trouble, now is the time to think logically. "Think logically" means that you do your own thinking rather than listen to suggestions from your peers. It requires you to use your common sense and take a few seconds to decide whether you want positive or negative consequences for yourself.

Sometimes it's easy to get so excited about friends' plans that we forget to think. Or we naively believe that *everyone's* going to be involved and that there's *no possibility* that we'll get caught. It's time to get real!

In order to **Make a Good Decision**, you must think about two substeps:

(A) Weigh Both Sides

(B) Decide: Stop or Go

(A) Weigh Both Sides

To make an intelligent decision for yourself, you need to **weigh both sides** of the situation. Ask yourself: "If I do this what *good* could happen? And if I do this, what *bad* could happen?" You may think that it will take you a long time to answer these questions. Actually, it won't, because your "pressuring" friend will already be telling you about all the good things that might happen. However, I bet that friend will not tell you about any bad things that might happen.

Why? Is your friend being intentionally mean? No—your friend just wants to pursue the activity and doesn't want to do it alone. Sometimes friends are scared of being caught and want someone to share the blame. We tend to think doing something is O.K. if more than one person does it, so your friend may be trying to gain confidence and rid him- or herself of guilt. It's also possible that your friend's self-esteem is low and he or she feels the need to impress you. "Showing off" gets a lot of people in trouble.

I've helped many teens look at trouble situations, and in every instance, if we looked at such a situation honestly, we found that at least twice as many bad things could happen as good. Rather poor odds.

Let's **weigh both sides** of a couple of situations.

Imagine that a friend asks you to skip the last class of the day because she's heard that the substitute teacher for the class is not checking roll. Your friend invites you to her house for a snack.

What good might happen? You may (1) have fun, (2) eat lots of snack food, (3) watch TV.

What bad might happen? (1) You may get caught leaving the school ground. (2) If so, your parents might receive a call from the school and (3) ground you or impose other punishment. (4) The rumor might be wrong—your regular teacher may be there and taking roll, so you still get caught, plus (5) you miss important classroom notes and maybe a pop test, which you flunk with a zero. (6) You also don't get the homework assignment. (7) Your friend's mother might come home early and catch you, in which case she may blame you for causing trouble and forbid her child to go places with you again. (8) If you get caught, you lose the trust of many adults.

In this next scenario, your friend complains that he had no time to finish his homework and wants to borrow your homework paper to copy.

What good might happen? (1) Your friend will be happy and like you. (2) Maybe you help the friend make a good grade. (3) Maybe someday the friend will return the favor.

What bad might happen? (1) Your friend may lose your paper. (2) You might get caught and both of you get a zero on the paper. (3) If so, you lose your teacher's trust, plus (4) you get embarrassed in class when the teacher catches you. (5) Even if the teacher doesn't actually catch you, realize that teachers usually know when this is going on. If you have been cheating, the teacher may not feel like giving you a break someday when you need one. (6) You may get caught and have to do the work over. (7) You might also get sent to the principal's office and (8) get detention. (9) If so, the principal may call your parents. (10) Your parents will probably take away some privileges and tell you not to see that friend anymore. (11) You lose your parent's trust. (12) Your friend might get caught and put the blame on you. (13) You really haven't helped your friend learn the homework material, so he flunks a test based on the homework. (14) If you don't get caught the first time, the friend will probably ask you to let him copy your homework again. (15) You may develop a reputation for loaning homework, and if so, other students will begin asking you for it. I'll stop here, although there are more negative possibilities.

Sometimes students say to me, "Sharon, everyone copies homework! It's no big deal! What's wrong with it?" My reply is "Well, besides the 15 possible outcomes listed above, it's just flat wrong. It's saying that the work that you turn in is yours, which is a lie. And if you feel sorry for your friend because he or she was too busy to do homework, consider that you friend had the same 24 hours to get the work done, just like you. It's not your responsibility that they wasted their time or were too busy. Besides, in the real adult world, you can get kicked out of college or fired from a job for cheating."

Let me give you two examples of cheating that I encountered as an adult within the last few years. I was conducting a training program at a county agency, and during a lunch break, one of its employees asked me to put the cost of her lunch on my check. She knew that the agency was paying for my meals and she wanted to get her lunch for free. She said no one would find out. Had I done this and had the department found out, the consequences for me would have included losing the contract to work for their agency, losing other work once the word got out that I "steal," and major embarrassment.

The second example occurred at a school where I was conducting inservice training for faculty members. The teachers were getting credits for attending my workshop. At the end of the day's training, I was asked by a teacher to sign an attendance form for her friend, who had left at lunch and was "too busy" to come back. Consequences for forging school records could have been severe. I used the Peer Pressure Reversal techniques outlined in this book to handle this situation, as well as the first one. Here, I used the "Act Shocked" technique, and in the first one I used the "Make an Excuse" technique. You will learn more about those techniques in Step 3.

I'm not lecturing to you. I just feel that it's important for all of us to decide early in life what kind of person that we want to be and take steps to achieve our goal. You can't cheat for years, then suddenly become an adult and say, "I'm going to stop now." It doesn't work that way. There are already too many people in the world who think that rules and laws are for everyone else, but not for them. This world would be friendlier, safer, and more orderly if we all tried to do what is right rather than what is easiest.

(B) Decide: Stop or Go

Now that you've looked at both sides of the situation, it's time to **decide** which way you'll act. Do you want to avoid potential trouble? Or are you willing to risk trouble? You must choose one, because if you don't make a firm decision then the friend will sense that you're unsure of yourself and may apply even more teasing and pressure. You can't be hesitant or you will be open to more manipulation.

Should you decide to risk trouble, you may not get caught right away. You may not get caught until the fourth time or maybe the seventh time you risk it, but the chances are, you *will* get caught sooner or later. And when you do get caught, be prepared for the consequences. The biggest consequence may be loss of freedom because adults won't think that you can handle tough decisions. As a result, they will make most of your decisions for you, which will make you feel like a little kid. Age does not guarantee that others will give you freedom and trust. Your decisions—depending on whether they're good or bad— give or take away your freedom.

Another negative consequence of risking trouble is guilt. You know when you've done wrong, and you may feel terrible about it. Guilt is a lousy way to feel.

When you decide to stop and avoid the trouble, not only do you benefit yourself, but you may help your friend, who probably won't pursue the trouble alone. If the friend is determined to follow through on the trouble anyway, then he or she may look for some "sucker" to convince. Just be glad that it's not you!

I've helped many school districts establish programs in peer helping. At the heart of the programs are peer helpers—students who are always on the alert, trying to **stop** trouble for themselves and others! These students actually serve as role models for making good decisions. They are usually highly respected kids who've already decided how they want to live their lives.

Let's apply **Decide: Stop or Go** to a couple of tricky situations.

We'll suppose you are a girl having lunch in the school cafeteria with some of your friends. One of them is talking about a new student named Tina. Your friend thinks Tina is stuck-up based on the way she dresses. Another friend says that she doesn't like her either—she thinks Tina's weird. They continue to cut the new student down. Then they ask what you think about Tina. Do you join in on this gossip, or what?

If you **decide** to get to know Tina before you judge her, then you've also decided to stop and not participate in the gossip. Of course, you may decide to stop for other reasons. Maybe you don't enjoy gossiping, even about people whom you don't like—you think it's a waste of time and in poor taste. Perhaps you've noticed that your friends seem to be jealous of almost any other girl, so you don't pay much attention to them when they talk about others— their insecurities are showing. Whatever your reasons, the important thing is that you make a good decision.

In this second scenario, we'll pretend that you are a guy spending the night over at a friend's house. The evening is fun until your friend suggests prank calling a teacher and hassling her. Your friend is mad at the teacher because he made a low grade in her class this week.

If you assess that this is trouble and plan to stop the situation from the get-go, then you've just used the **Decide** substep. Making the phone call definitely spells trouble as it breaks a law, could scare a teacher whom *you* like, and could be subject to discipline by parents should they find out.

In summary, it takes confidence and strength to **make good decisions**. But, honestly, who do you want to do your thinking for you? Will it be your friends, or yourself? None of us likes to admit that we let our friends influence us, but it happens all the time. It even happens to adults. Some people select colleges based on where their friends are going, rather than on what university might be best for their career plans. Some people get married because they've dated someone a long time and their friends expect them to marry; they give little thought to whether they actually want to spend the rest of their life with this person. Some couples have kids because of pressure from relatives

It can be weird out there—everyone trying to poke their noses into our business! That's why I want us all to become independent thinkers!

```
┌────────────────────────────────────────────┐
│                                              │
│   DON'T JUST FIT IN  ➜  STAND OUT!           │
│                                              │
└────────────────────────────────────────────┘
```

PPR STEP 3:
ACT TO AVOID TROUBLE

Step 3, **Act to Avoid Trouble**, is the most important of the three PPR steps. The first two steps have prepared you for this step. Now you need to follow through on your decision and avoid being controlled. You need to say or do something that will let your friends know that you are not going to join them. And you must do this in 30 seconds or less. These **actions to avoid trouble** can be diplomatic, dramatic, smooth, friendly, strong, nice, aloof, or whatever you want or need them to be in order to handle the situation. It's up to you to decide which ones to use and how to use them. They will get you out of a trouble trap, helping you *reverse* the peer pressure and keep your friends at the same time.

These are the two substeps of **Act to Avoid Trouble**:

(A) What to Say

(B) How to Say It

(A) What to Say

People who have good communication skills think quickly. They usually weren't born that way. Generally they practiced a lot to become better communicators. Good communicators are not only interesting and fun to be with, but also capable of preventing others from influencing them in negative ways. They seem to have responses in their back pocket.

I want you, too, to have responses in your back pocket that you can whip out at a moment's notice in order to make good decisions for yourself. When you "hem and haw," think too slowly, act unsure of yourself, or present yourself as a weak person, others may take advantage of you. That can get you into trouble. You're also a likely candidate for getting into trouble if you want so badly to be cool that you'll do practically anything that others ask of you. Knowing **what to say** helps *you* set the standard for what's *really* cool.

Below are 10 PPR choices of **what to say** to avoid trouble. Why so many choices? Because people have different personality styles, and so prefer different responses. You must find those that suit your style. And in most peer pressure situations, it will take more than one to comfortably get yourself out of harm's way. Start thinking about which styles fit *your* personality.

THE 10 PPR RESPONSES

1. **Simply Say No**
2. **Leave the Scene**
3. **Ignore the Peer(s)**
4. **Make an Excuse**
5. **Change the Subject**
6. **Make a Joke**
7. **Act Shocked**
8. **Use Flattery**
9. **Suggest a Better Idea**
10. **Return the Challenge**

Let's look at these responses one by one.

1. Simply Say No

This is a basic response that should perhaps be used more often. It's simple, upfront, honest, direct, and courageous. It can be done politely or firmly—depending on how much pressure you are under. The important point is to keep it short and closed to further discussion. Your tone of voice and the look on your face as you say it can tell your friends exactly how you feel about their invitation to trouble.

You can probably think of other ways to **simply say no**, but here's a start:

Shake your head.	"Uh-uh."
"No thank you."	"I'd rather not."
"No way!"	"That's dumb."
"I'll pass."	"Don't want to."
"Not if I want to live."	"Are you crazy?"
"Can't."	"Nope."
"When pigs fly!"	"Thanks, but no thanks."
"That's wrong."	"Forget it!"
"I'm not really interested."	"Not if I want to see
"Definitely not."	tomorrow."
"No way, José!"	"Maybe next year—
"Never in a million years."	remember to ask me."
"Don't get your hopes up."	"Forget it, Fred."
"I would if I could, but I	"Sorry, Charlie."
can't and I won't."	"Count me out."
"Not me!"	"Read my lips—no!"

You can also use the "broken record" approach by repeating the same phrase over and over until your friend gets frustrated, finally gets the message, and gives up. For example, if your friend asks you to stay out later than your curfew, you say, "I can't." As your friend continues to beg, you keep saying, "I can't" until he or she takes the hint.

For kicks, you can learn to say the word "no" in several foreign languages, such as *nyet* in Russian, *nein* in German, *ne* in Czech, and *non* in French!

If your friend keeps on, you can always ask, "What part of the word 'no' do you not understand?"

SIMPLY SAY NO...

2. Leave the Scene

It has been said that actions speak louder than words. To indicate your disapproval of the invitation or to avoid continuing to argue with a friend, you might choose to just walk away. **Leaving** can be done in a friendly manner (shaking your head in disbelief and laughing as you walk away) or briskly (hurriedly leaving serious trouble that may happen momentarily). You don't need to explain yourself—you just need to convey, in action, that you have better things to do. If you're **leaving** a large group, the kids in it probably won't even notice your exit.

To avoid being teased, you must walk away without looking scared (head and eyes downcast) and without appearing to be a snob (nose stuck up in the air and prissing away). You must never do the "yo-yo," which is leaving but then returning when the others tempt you with more information. When you walk back to the person offering trouble, you appear interested. Once you **leave**, you must keep going and stay away. If you need to say anything as you walk away, turn your head and say it over your shoulder. Should your friends try to block your exit, just spin around them and keep moving forward. Don't shove. In fact, keep your arms down at your sides and keep talking so that you appear friendly but determined. Your momentum should carry you on your way.

So how do you **leave** correctly? Just normally. Keep your head up, look straight ahead, and move fairly quickly. You want to appear *decisive*, like you know what you're doing (whether you really do or not!). And, if you want to add flair to your departure, learn to say "goodbye" in several languages, such as *Auf Wiedersehen* in German, *adíos* in Spanish, *au revoir* in French, and *sayonara* in Japanese!

Remember to **leave** any time you are being asked to break a law, because if you stay you could get arrested for being an accomplice. Also remember that when you are outnumbered, meaning that more friends want to go along with the trouble than not, then it is important to **leave** quickly. In fact, cut the departure time to 15 seconds so you don't give the group the opportunity to hassle you!

Finally, if you have tried other PPR techniques of saying no and your friend is still on your back, then you must **leave the scene**. The rule is that you say "no" no more than twice before you walk away. You may have several PPR responses within your reply, but overall there should be no more than two attempts to make it clear that you don't want to join your friend. Why? Because if you take too long to handle the trouble, you will either be convinced to go along with it or you will get in a major argument with your friend. Both can be avoided by getting away from the pressuring peer.

DON'T FORGET!

The Leave the Scene Rule Is . . .

*Say "no," using any PPR responses, no more than **twice** before you end the discussion and walk away.*

LEAVE THE SCENE...

3. Ignore the Peer(s)

Another PPR technique is to **ignore** your friend's comment or suggestion. I also call this the "airhead" approach, as you must appear that you don't know what's going on—that you are distracted by something, are involved in some activity, or you just didn't hear your friend. You can pretend to be busy studying, deep in thought, listening to another conversation, or taking notes. Another possible tactic, one you can use at school, is to simply get up and go sharpen your pencil.

This PPR response can be used effectively in the classroom when someone is asking you for an answer during a test, wants you to pass a note, or wants to carry on a conversation with you during the teacher's lecture. Even if you only replied, "Shh, we're not supposed to be talking," you could get in trouble if the teacher looks up as you say it. If you **ignore** the friend, he or she will either get caught (instead of you!) or get the hint and give up in frustration. Later in the hall, be friendly and say, "I want to talk to you, but not during the test! Sit with me at lunch, O.K.?"

Ignoring is also helpful when you want to avoid a situation where gossip and rumors are being discussed. This world would be a nicer place for us all if we focused on what's nice about others rather than wasted our time hashing over each others' faults.

Yet another time that **ignoring** can prove helpful is when you know someone's middle name is Trouble and you choose to avoid coming in contact with that person!

IGNORE THE PEER...

4. Make an Excuse

Making an excuse is the favorite PPR response among teens because a person can avoid actually saying no to a friend. Realize, however, that it is not mandatory that you explain the reason why you're turning down your friend's invitation. It's really *your* business if you don't want to take part in the trouble. But if you'll feel more comfortable using an **excuse** than saying no, then go for it!

Make sure your **excuse** is truthful because lying is a bad habit and may result in your losing a friend if the lie is discovered. There are always lots of **true excuses** that you can use—things that you could or should be doing, including:

"I've got to finish my chores."

"I've got lots of homework to do."

"I just got off being grounded and don't want to take any chances."

"My parents would kill me!"

"I need to help with dinner" (or "with the yard" and so forth).

"I have to watch my baby brother."

"I've got to go to _____" (soccer practice, piano lessons, football practice, and so forth).

"I have to check in with my parents" (or "my boyfriend").

"I need to clean my room."

"I've got to go to work shortly."

Excuses can be less specific, such as "I've got other plans," "I'm busy," or "I don't feel like it." You could also say that your friend's suggestion doesn't sound like fun.

One sure-fire way to get a friend off your back is to give this **excuse**: "I *always* get caught! Take me along and we'll all get in trouble!" Another effective **excuse** is to go to the bathroom. It's unlikely that your friend will follow you *there* to continue pressuring you!

MAKE AN EXCUSE...

5. Change the Subject

Those of you who are "chatterboxes" can always **change the subject** when your friend suggests trouble. You like to talk and do it naturally. Well, use that talent when you most need it! Think of something that your friend is really interested in—cars, movies, sports, guys or girls—and begin a lengthy discussion of it. This involves quick thinking and fast talking.

Here are some examples of easy and effective ways to **change the subject**:

"Guess what I heard about you? It's all over the school."

Your friend will probably be curious and ask, "What did you hear?" Your reply can be something like, "John said you were good in science," or "John said you were nice." You pass on a nice, *truthful* compliment while also diverting your friend from the trouble.

"What are you going to wear to the dance next month?"

Girls generally like to discuss clothes, and bringing up the subject may make your friend forget about her trouble idea.

"Did you watch the game Sunday? Wow, four interceptions!"

Lots of guys are into sports, and they'll probably forget about the trouble idea when you start to talk about their favorite sport.

Once you've got your friend on another subject, keep the conversation fast-paced to avoid falling back on the trouble idea. Your friend will most likely know that you intentionally changed the subject, and that's okay. It's your way of handling the situation without coming right out and saying no.

CHANGE THE SUBJECT...

6. Make a Joke

If you have a good sense of humor, then you will like the technique of **making a joke**. Saying no in a funny or silly manner can be a great way to express your "no" message while showing your friend that you still like him or her. It can lighten the atmosphere and everyone likes it. You don't have to be a master comedian like Sinbad, Jay Leno, Ellen Degeneres, Eddie Murphy, or Paul Rodriquez. You just need to develop some fun, playful responses ahead of time that you can whip out at a moment's notice.

My sense of humor is corny, as are some of the following lines. If you are *really* a natural comedian, then you can make up some much better lines! Write me with your ideas!

When asked to go somewhere that you shouldn't, you could reply . . .

"Love to, but I've already made plans. I've got to go home and rearrange my underwear drawer!"

"Rats, that's the same night as my Hollywood screen test."

"Can't. I promised my gerbil that I'd rollerblade with him after school!"

"I'm in my comfort zone and unable to leave."

"I have to go to the post office. I've got to check to see if I'm still on a wanted poster."

"I've got to stay home and inflate my date."

"Mission Control. Your order is to abort the mission. Come back to base."

When you're asked to do something you shouldn't,
say . . .

"Are you kidding? If I did that, my reputation might
improve!"

"I've recently entered a contest. I'm trying to win the
prize for the person who goes the longest without
saying yes."

"I never go out on days that end in *y*."

"I'm running off to Yugoslavia with a foreign exchange
student named Basil Metabolism."

"I can't leave home until I learn if my patent-pending
permit has been approved."

Another way to turn down a trouble invitation is to
put down the idea. Normally you don't want to put down
your friend, but normally (I hope) your friend doesn't try to
involve you in trouble! Responses like the ones below help
you do this in a joking fashion, conveying the message
"That's really dumb and you know better."

"That idea is one taco short of a combination plate."

"The lights are on, but no one's at home."

"That's two cinder blocks short of a dorm!"

"Your elevator isn't going all the way to the top today!"

"I think you don't have all of your oars in the water!"

"You're not playing with a full deck right now."

Another way to **joke** your way out of trouble is to "play dumb." When a friend suggests trouble, ask, "I'm sorry but I don't get it. What exactly do you want to do and why?" Your friend will probably explain the trouble plan more carefully. Then say, "This is really confusing. What is it you want me to do? Explain it slower, please." A patient friend might answer you one more time, at which time you say, "This just doesn't make sense. I don't get it. Go over this just one more time." At this point your frustrated friend will probably say, "Just forget it." You reply, "O.K." Instead of playing it *dumb*, you played it *smart*!

Be creative with the **joke** technique. It's a fun one!

MAKE A JOKE...

7. Act Shocked

Acting shocked allows you to act as if you can't believe what you just heard your friend ask! You can act amazed, surprised, and even disbelieving! You can be dramatic and theatrical on this one if you want. Roll your eyes, let your mouth drop open, and say, "I can't believe what you just said. You must be joking!"

This PPR response has at least two clear advantages. It gives your friend an easy way out of the situation too: if your friend is having second thoughts about the trouble suggestion, he or she can reply, "Yeah, I was just kidding. I just wanted to see what you'd say!" It also very politely expresses just how strongly you don't want to go along with the dumb idea.

There are a number of other ways to communicate the **Act Shocked** response, including:

"Do you know how much trouble you would get into?
   I won't let you even discuss this further."

"I *know* you really didn't mean that."

"Yeah, sure, just what I always wanted to do!"

"How silly! Earth calling (your friend's name)."

"How did I pick such a goofy friend? Just lucky,
   I guess!"

"Are you crazy?"

"You really didn't say that. There must be a ventriloquist
   in the house."

"Where do you get your ideas—from 'Looney Tunes' on
   Saturday morning?"

Act Shocked is the PPR response that I often use with my peers. It has never failed me.

ACT SHOCKED...

8. Use Flattery

Flattery can get you somewhere—right out of a tight spot! This technique calls for you to express to your friend that he or she is really too smart (or nice) to follow through with the trouble idea. Few of us get enough compliments and everyone likes to hear this line used on them. Use of this technique will not only keep you out of trouble but strongly encourage your friend to do the same.

Flattery examples include the following:

"You're too smart to really mean that."

"This isn't one of your all-time great ideas! Come on, let's do a little better."

"You're too good a friend for me to let you do that."

"You always think of such good ideas. Think of one now that won't get us grounded forever."

"If we got caught doing this, it would mess up our weekend plans. No way!"

"You know better than that!"

This technique is especially good to use with best friends and boyfriends or girlfriends.

USE FLATTERY...

9. Suggest a Better Idea

This easy PPR technique for avoiding trouble requires no special skills; you just have to think of something different to do that would be O.K. The **Suggest a Better Idea** response strengthens your friendship because you're including your friend in the solution to the situation. You're ignoring his or her bad idea and substituting an activity that would be fun but not get either of you in trouble.

Propose your **better idea** with a smile and an enthusiastic voice. This is using *positive* peer pressure. You are guiding your friend toward safe, legal alternatives.

It's simple to introduce your **better ideas**—just use these phrases:

"I've got a great idea! Let's _____."
(Fill in the blank with interesting things to do, such as rollerblading, shooting baskets, learning tennis, and listening to a new CD.)

"Why don't we _____ instead?"
(Consider activities that your friend would like to do: shopping, looking at a teen magazine, practicing a new dance, getting something to eat, or going to a movie.)

There are lots of **better ideas** that you could suggest. Be enthusiastic about them! If you act bored, your friend may find it easy to take control of the plans and suggest yet another trouble idea to impress you and any other friends present. *Always* be involved in the plans and offer fun and safe suggestions.

SUGGEST A BETTER IDEA...

10. Return the Challenge

Occasionally a friend will try hard to pressure you with words. He or she may taunt you with unkind words, call your mother names, threaten not to be your friend, or generally try to intimidate or make fun of you. Realize that the friend's goal is control—to do what he or she wants to do. Rarely will young people pursue trouble by themselves, but if someone else is along for support or to show off in front of, they'll often badger that person to join them.

When the friend ignores your PPR responses and keeps pressuring you, it's time for you to get tough, not by fighting but by learning to defend yourself with words. You must develop a high level of communication skills to manage the dares and challenges of others, but I know you're up to it!

It's similar to playing tennis. When a friend serves to you, you try to slam the ball back into his or her court. Well, when a friend dares you, you must return the dare right back to him or her.

The worst thing you can do (which is what most of us do) is to become defensive. We may respond by yelling back at our friends or calling them names too. What a great way to start a fistfight or to lose the friend! Remember, our goal is to be able to say no when it's needed, yet still keep our friends.

An example of being defensive is answering, "No I'm not!" when a friend taunts you, saying "Chicken!" Your answer backs you into a corner because the friend will retaliate with "Then prove it! Do it!" Most of us would stomp off and do it just to show the friend we're not afraid. Look who's in control. The friend! *By using words*, he or she got us to do something that we didn't even want to do. Our lack of quick thinking and good comebacks weakened our position, and so we made a poor decision.

So let's learn some ways to **return the challenge**.

When a friend says, "I thought you were my friend. If you were, you'd do this with me," you can use one of several comebacks:

"I *am* your friend. And that's why I'm *not* going to do this with you."

"If you were *my* friend, then you'd get off my back when I say no."

"With friends like you, who needs enemies? Stop trying to get me in trouble!"

"Best friends don't try to boss each other around. Please let me do my own thinking."

If you're friend is being really unkind and pushy, a stinging zinger is . . .

"Who said you were my friend?" (You can soften it, if desired, by laughing.)

When a friend taunts you with "Chicken," "Mama's baby," "Scaredy cat," "Wimp," and other such confidence-busting names, use one of these possible comebacks to "save face":

"Thanks, I'm really glad you noticed. I'm so proud of it."
"Yep!"
"So?"
"It takes one to know one." (Use this one carefully. In certain situations it would start a fight.)
"Anybody smart would be."
"I'd rather be a chicken than a dead duck." (It's an old line, but still O.K.!)
"I know you are, but what am I?"
"What's wrong with chickens? Personally, I've always thought they're O.K.!"

You also can toss the "hot potato" right back when dared with "Are you chicken?" by saying, "Are you scared to do it by yourself?" If your friend answers "No," then say, "Then prove it! But I think you know better." And walk away. Now the dare is off you and back on your friend. You've been nice and friendly but stayed out of trouble. Some people might wonder if you're trying to talk your friend into trouble. No way! You're just trying to get the friend off your case. And as I've mentioned before, he or she probably won't pursue the trouble alone. So you may have helped your friend. If the friend is dead set on causing trouble, then he or she will find another person to do it with. Ultimately, you can't control what you friend does, only what *you* do.

Let's look at another possible outcome. Suppose you ask your friend "Are you afraid to do it alone?" and he or she truthfully answers "Yes." How do you respond in turn? By saying, "Good, so am I. Let's think of something else to do." Then you **suggest a better idea**! In this way, you get off the topic of trouble quickly. And because you've shown your approval of your friend's honesty and let him or her know that you're scared to cause trouble too, your friend won't feel like a jerk. In fact, he or she will probably feel more confident about making good decisions in the future and be happy to have a *real* friend like you.

You might be wondering, But what if a *group* is daring me? A situation like that may be difficult to handle, but it's not impossible. Just change the comeback question a little. Ask: "You mean *you guys* can't do this without me? I'm sure you can. Have fun if you do it, and I hope you don't get caught." The response will still work with more than one person.

RETURN THE CHALLENGE...

(B) How to Say It

You've learned *what* to say when faced with negative peer pressure; now let's talk about **how to say it**. Actions sometimes speak louder than words, so it is important to appear confident and in control as you use the 10 PPR zingers.

It doesn't matter if you don't *feel* confident when handling trouble. Few of us do. But you want to *look* cool and collected. Never let them see you sweat!

To look confident, firm, and in control, you must first "stand tall." This involves standing or sitting with your back straight. You should "square off" with the person you're talking to, which just means to face him or her. Avoid nervous gestures like clearing your throat frequently, slouching, wringing your hands, walking away backwards (if you leave, then turn and do it), bending your head down, shuffling around, or avoiding eye contact.

It's critical that you make eye contact with the pressuring peer (the only exception is when you are trying to *ignore* the friend). Eye contact needs to be maintained. Don't stare or glare—just look at the friend as you both continue to talk.

To *sound* confident, you should speak in a clear, firm voice. If you whisper, "I don't think so," your friend will surely keep pressuring you. You're presenting yourself as weak. You look easy to persuade and about to give in. On the other hand, if you shout at your friend, you could start an argument.

Along with looking and sounding confident, it's *essential* that you apply the **30-Second Rule**: once you've identified that you're being asked to go along with trouble, get out of the situation or away from the peer within 30 seconds.

In this way, you don't give your friend enough time to pressure you into changing your decision, and you avoid getting into an argument or a fight. So forget about debating the issue! That will take too long and your friend will simply increase the pressure. Instead, focus on dealing with the situation the PPR way. Quickly draw on one or two of the 10 PPR responses; then, if your friend doesn't back down, end the discussion and **leave the scene**. Examples of what to say:

"I'm not going to discuss this with you any more. Bye."
"You didn't take the hint. I've told you no twice. End of
     conversation." (You walk away.)
"I told you I'd leave if you didn't stop this discussion.
     That time's here. So long."
"If you don't want to talk about something else, well
     maybe somebody else will. See ya."

REMEMBER!

The 30-Second Rule Is . . .
Get out of the peer pressure situation in 30 seconds or less.

AND DON'T FORGET!

The Leave the Scene Rule Is . . .
*Say "no," using any PPR responses, no more than **twice** before you end the discussion and walk away.*

Which of the 10 PPR responses fit your personality best? My personal favorites are **Act Shocked, Make a Joke**, and **Return the Challenge**. Those suit my style the best. It's important for you to decide on some favorites because you'll need to recall them fast when peer pressure arises. And in most peer pressure situations, you'll need more than one to comfortably get out of the situation. So it's good to have at least three or four that you really like.

Let's see if we can put PPR into practice as we take a look at the stories in the next chapter.

4.

PPR

IN ACTION

(LIGHTS, CAMERA,

ACTION!)

SCENE 1

On the way home from school, Shawn and Jeremy have stopped at a convenience store for a soft drink.

As Shawn starts to count the money in his pocket, he says, "Rats, I'm starving and I don't have enough money for a soda *and* candy."

Jeremy replies, "No big deal. Just take the candy, man. I do it all the time. The clerk can't see us all the way back here."

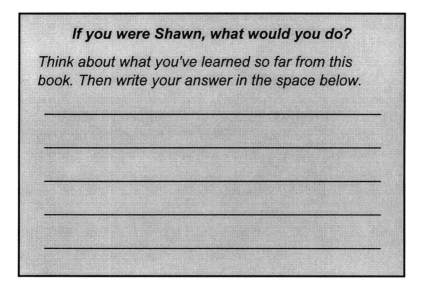

If you were Shawn, what would you do?

Think about what you've learned so far from this book. Then write your answer in the space below.

Shawn's Responses

Shawn **checks out the scene** and notices that Jeremy is acting nervous and whispering, so he knows that this is trouble. He also knows that stealing is wrong, so he **decides** not to do it. As he tries to think of **what to say or do**, he knows there are many PPR options, including **Simply Say No**, **Leave the Scene**, and **Act Shocked**.

Shawn decides to be gutsy and says, "**No way!** That's a dumb idea and you know it. **I'm not about to go to jail over a candy bar!**"

Jeremy says, "But we won't get caught . . ."

Shawn interrupts him with, "Yeah, we're not going to get caught because we're not going to do it! **Let's go pay for our sodas.** Come on, Jer!"

Jeremy mumbles that it would have been easy, but follows Shawn, who is **walking briskly up to the cash register**.

Shawn not only helped himself but a friend as well by **saying no**, **acting shocked**, **making an excuse**, **suggesting a better idea**, and **leaving the scene**. Shawn's gutsy approach fueled his self-confidence. He was even able to say no directly while delivering his **Excuse** and **Act Shocked** responses! Notice how *quickly* he took control of the situation and *kept* it. He handled the invitation to trouble like a pro. You can too!

SCENE 2

Katy and Mandy are attending a slumber party at Shannon's house. It's Shannon's birthday and they've had lots of fun listening to music, eating snacks, and talking on the phone with friends. Katy reminds her friends that a movie they want to watch on TV is coming on.

Mandy grins at Shannon and says, "Oh, we forgot to tell you about our surprise plan."

Katy says, "What's up? I love surprises!"

Shannon replies, "Well, you know those cute brothers that live down the street. They're names are K.C. and Nick Pepper. We're going to sneak out of the house. My parents are already asleep. We'll go knock on their bedroom window and talk to them for a few minutes."

Katy asks, "What if your parents wake up?"

Shannon assures her that they won't.

If you were Katy, what would you do?

This situation is especially tough because Katy is outnumbered. Two friends want to pursue the trouble and she doesn't. Still, there are ways to handle the situation. If you were Katy, how would you handle it?

Think about what you've learned so far from this book. Then write your answer in the space on the next page.

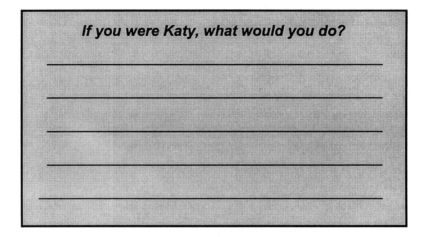

If you were Katy, what would you do?

_____

_____

_____

_____

_____

Katy's Responses

Katy quickly **weighs both sides** of the situation. On one hand, it would be fun to talk to these cute guys. On the other hand, she and her friends could get caught; then her parents would find out and she would be grounded. She also knows that it would be a long time before she would be trusted to spend the night away from home again, plus she might be forbidden to see Mandy and Shannon. Another thought that crosses her mind is that it's really late and sneaking around the neighborhood could be dangerous. Katy also wonders what the guys will think about her and her friends seeing them in such a secretive way. The guys might get the wrong impression. Katy knows she must not go, so she says, **"Why don't we just call the guys and talk to them on the phone."**

Mandy and Shannon both say that it would be much more fun to see them in person. Katy agrees, but adds, **"You both know our parents would kill us if they found out. Besides, the guys might get the wrong idea and then we'd really be in a mess."**

Shannon comes on stronger: "It's my party and I say we all go."

Katy answers, **"You two go on if you have to.** I hope you don't get caught. **I'm just going to stay here** and watch this movie I've been dying to see."

Mandy and Shannon go to the kitchen to discuss the situation. Shannon's mom suddenly walks into the kitchen. She says, "That pizza made me thirsty. I'm going to get some juice. Having fun, girls?"

Shannon says, "Yes, the movie just started. We're going to pop some popcorn."

Her mother goes back to bed. Mandy and Shannon decide eating popcorn is really a good idea. They walk back into the den, where Katy is engrossed in the movie. No one even mentions the plans to sneak out.

Katy did a great job handling the trouble. Which of the 10 PPR responses did she use? She **suggested a better idea**, **made excuses**, and also **returned the challenge.**

SCENE 3

Jay and Cedric are walking to their last class of the day. Jay excitedly says, "Guess what I heard? There's a substitute teacher in this class and she's not checking roll. Let's hop in my car and go to my house. We can kick back and have a sandwich. You in?"

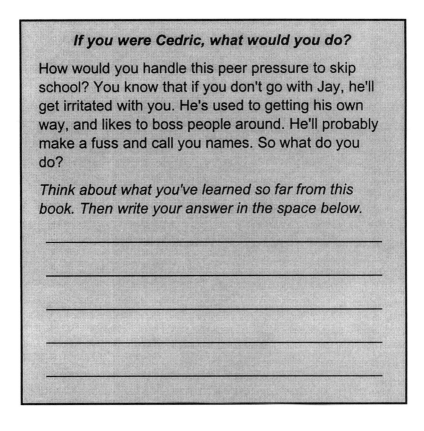

If you were Cedric, what would you do?

How would you handle this peer pressure to skip school? You know that if you don't go with Jay, he'll get irritated with you. He's used to getting his own way, and likes to boss people around. He'll probably make a fuss and call you names. So what do you do?

Think about what you've learned so far from this book. Then write your answer in the space below.

_____

_____

_____

_____

_____

Cedric's Responses

Cedric thinks fast as he notices a cute girl, Casey, walking into class. He says to Jay, **"Hey, I've got to go talk to Casey about a really important matter. I'll come over after school for a sandwich. See you later."** Cedric walks quickly into the classroom and strikes up a conversation with Casey.

The PPR responses that Cedric chose to use were **Ignore the Peer(s)** and **Suggest a Better Idea**. Cedric also applied the **Leave the Scene Rule**. He really played it cool. A minute later, he also noticed that Jay had walked into class and taken a seat. Apparently Jay couldn't find a willing victim.

SCENE 4

Two guys, Alexander and Scott, are at the school dance. Not many students have dates. Everybody decided to make it a casual occasion and not go in pairs. The guys notice two girls whom they want to meet. They've seen the girls in the hall, but don't know their names.

They decide to go over and ask the girls to dance. Mitzi and Tiff (the two girls) accept. After the song ends, Alexander says, "Why don't you two come outside with us. We've got some beer stashed away."

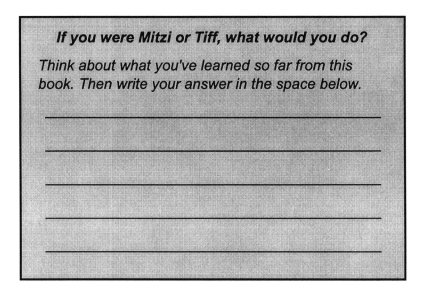

If you were Mitzi or Tiff, what would you do?

Think about what you've learned so far from this book. Then write your answer in the space below.

Mitzi's and Tiff's Responses

Mitzi answers, "**But if we leave the dance, we won't be allowed to come back in.**"

"That's O.K." Scott says. "I've got my car and we can go driving around."

Tiff replies, "**Just what I've *always* wanted to do— ride around in a car with someone drinking. A good friend of mine, Shelly, died that way. C'mon, guys, let's stay at the dance and have fun here. We both hate the taste of beer anyway.**"

Mitzi says, "**Ooh, there's a slow dance!** My favorite song! **Alexander, let's dance.**"

As they walk off to dance, Scott says, "I'm really sorry about your friend. I don't care much about beer either. I guess we were just trying to impress you two."

Tiff replies, "**Scott, you impress me; what you drink doesn't.**"

They look at each other for a minute and then begin to dance.

Mitzi and Tiff handled this situation well. Mitzi **made an excuse**, then quickly **suggested a better idea**. Tiff **made a joke** (though it was more sarcastic than funny) and **suggested a better idea**. She also shared her personal experience of losing a friend to drinking and driving (a powerful form of **making an excuse**) and **used flattery** to reinforce Scott's concern and honesty.

Scene 5

Felicia, Maria, Antoinette, and LaShonda are sitting in the cafeteria eating lunch. Felicia and Antoinette are putting down another girl, Lauren, who sometimes sits with them at lunch.

Felicia says, "Lauren has no taste at all. I wouldn't be caught dead in the stuff she wears."

Antoinette laughs and adds, "And she walks with her nose stuck up in the air. What a snob! I hope she doesn't sit with us today. Maria, put your books on that empty seat. If she comes over, tell her someone's already sitting there."

LaShonda says, "She's done nothing to us. Why are you dissing her so bad?"

Felicia says, "You don't like her either, do you, Maria? I don't know why LaShonda is acting so goody-two-shoes today."

If you were Maria, what would you do?
If you were LaShonda, what would you do?

This is a tacky gossip situation that calls for some PPR action. How would you handle it? First pretend you're Maria; then LaShonda.

Think about what you've learned so far from this book. Then write your answer in the space on the next page.

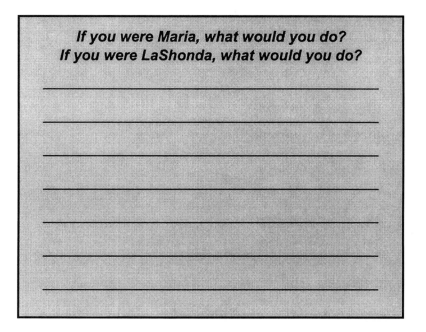

If you were Maria, what would you do?
If you were LaShonda, what would you do?

Maria's and LaShonda's Responses

Maria, who had time to check out this situation, **ignored** Felicia's question and said, "Lauren has been eating lunch with us most of the year. **Why are you on her case today? Is it because she made such a good grade in science and we didn't?** There's no reason to be jealous. If we all stayed off the phone more, we could make good grades like she does."

Antoinette tried to deny what Maria had said. "No, I don't care what grade she makes. She just shouldn't brag about it."

Maria replied, "*She* didn't brag. The teacher bragged on her."

"That's true," LaShonda added. "Besides, Lauren has been nice to work with us on our homework when we don't understand it. **Let's change the subject.**" She looked down at her cafeteria food and said, "**Umm, great mashed potatoes, huh?**"

The girls all laughed. The responses in this peer pressure situation are a bit complicated, as both Maria and LaShonda not only refused to "diss" Lauren but also rallied to her defense. Maria also refused to turn on LaShonda, first **ignoring** Felicia's comment about LaShonda ("goody-two-shoes") and question about Lauren ("You don't like her either, do you, Maria?"), then using a form of **Return the Challenge.** LaShonda in turn backs up Maria's defense of Lauren, then **changes the subject** and **makes a joke.**

Together, Maria and LaShonda worked nicely to divert the peer pressure and to show that *they* were not scared of Lauren's success. Knowing how to deal well with this kind of peer pressure is important, because it's rooted in the fear of other people's success, and that fear is becoming more common. Some people who are afraid they can't do something (or are too lazy to try) put down others who do work hard or receive an honor. Don't ever do less than your best because you're afraid of teasing or being called a "brain." Those who apply themselves are the ones who will be successful in life.

5.

TOBACCO,

ALCOHOL,

OTHER DRUGS,

SEX,

AND VIOLENCE

This is a special section devoted to five highly important topics: tobacco, alcohol, other drugs, sex, and violence. These are often the target areas of negative peer pressure, and a person who makes poor decisions when pressured to become involved in them can suffer severe consequences, including the loss of his or her life. I will discuss them very seriously, for all across our country, young adults, teens, and preteens are being encouraged by friends to risk their health, safety, and self-esteem. A lot of adults, too, are taking such risks, losing their careers, marriages, and self-respect because of poor decisions in these areas. We fail to evaluate the consequences realistically and think we are invincible.

We're not. I travel frequently in my work and hear countless stories of good, well-meaning people, like you, who either get hurt, get into serious trouble, get arrested, or die because of poor choices in these areas. At some time in your life, someone is going to ask you to become involved in one or more of these activities. Let's get prepared with the facts about, and the skills to resist, these most damaging activities.

USE OF TOBACCO

Some young people think that smoking cigarettes or cigars or using smokeless tobacco (snuff and chewing tobacco) makes them look grown-up and sophisticated. If you think smoking will give you social status, please think again. Actually, smokers look like a chimney and smell worse. Those that use snuff and chewing tobacco drool, spit a lot, and have a face that looks out of shape.

When I was single, I never would date a smoker because he would smell so bad. And to kiss a smoker—ugh!—like licking an ashtray! Even my dogs don't like the smell of cigarettes! Once we were out walking and one of my dogs, Nicholas, trotted up to a woman who happened to be smoking. Nicholas had never seen a cigarette before and sniffed to see what it was. He began snorting, sneezed, then rubbed his nose on the ground, then snorted some more. It was hilarious! I often wonder why we aren't as smart as my dog. No way would he ever smoke!

This is one area about which kids can learn something from adults. Adults are paying millions of dollars to doctors for treatment, hypnosis, patches, gum, and so forth to try to get rid of this addictive habit. They have become ill from smoking, seen friends and relatives die from it, know they stink from it, and find fewer and fewer locations where they're allowed to do it; yet they still have difficulty breaking the habit! It's sad to see some people actually *run* off a plane that just landed to find a place where they can smoke. Their bodies actually hurt because they aren't giving it the nicotine that it craves.

Every relative in my family who failed to quit using tobacco has already died from it—from either heart disease, emphysema, or lung cancer. I know a lot about these diseases because I've spent a lot of time in the hospital with these dying relatives. It was a terribly painful death for these people—all still relatively young— and horrible for me and other family members to watch. The warning labels on tobacco products don't begin to describe the suffering and pain.

In March 1997, one of the five U.S. cigarette makers agreed to cooperate with 22 state attorney generals in their lawsuits against the tobacco industry for billions of dollars in smoking-related Medicaid claims. After years of denial they finally admitted that cigarettes are addictive and cause cancer and heart disease. They also acknowledged that the tobacco industry targets children through its advertising. It appears they knew cigarettes were harmful back in the 1970s, but apparently tried to hide the research from the public. Think about it. Do you want to give *your* money to people who did not make sure their product was 100 percent safe for the buyer? And who apparently knew it was *dangerous* for the buyer, but couldn't have cared less?

If you use tobacco, or are thinking of using it, you'd probably like to say to me: "But Sharon, I don't (or won't) smoke *that* much. And I'll quit as soon as _____" ("I get married"; "I have kids"; "I get past final exams"; "I start feeling lousy"; "I can find a friend to quit with me"; "I lose 5 pounds"; or "I don't have so much pressure in my life"). I've heard all these excuses and more. *Older smokers will tell you that they used these excuses too and one day realized that years had gone by and they were still smoking!* Even if you only smoke two cigarettes a day, you leave yourself open to those times when stress and other factors will make you crave more. And once you reach that pack-a-day level (the level of the average smoker), you're usually hooked at that level (and very vulnerable to smoking even more cigarettes a day).

If you don't smoke that much, be happy that your decision to quit right now won't be as difficult to follow through on as it would be years from now. If you don't smoke now, don't start. You haven't needed it so far, so why develop a need for it? If nothing else, think of all the better things you can do with your money. And if your friends are pressuring you to smoke because it's "cool," just hang in there and remain firm in your decision. The chances are, they'll become used to your being a nonsmoker and leave you alone about it. Also, it's possible these same friends will be saying to you years from now, "Man, I wish I'd taken a cue from you." Talk to older smokers some time, and you'll find out how well they remember the one or two kids in their crowd who didn't smoke, and how much they in retrospect envy those kids for not starting!

Look at some of the facts:

1. American teens spend over **$1 billion** a year on tobacco. (What a waste of money! Think of all the CDs, TVs, clothes, or cars that would buy! Or think of what good these teens could do if they donated even a little of this money to their favorite charity—what a difference it could make!)

2. 75 percent of all teens do **not** use tobacco. (Here is one area where positive peer pressure should be an encouragement.)

3. 60 percent of Americans who smoke started smoking by the time they were 14 years old; an additional 20 percent begin smoking between the ages of 15 and 21. (Very few people begin this habit when they are older!)

4. According to the World Health Organization, **one person dies every 10 seconds** as a result of tobacco use. (That statistic does **not** include fatalities due to passive smoking. According to the American Cancer Society's Prevention II Study, if you live with a smoker but are not one yourself, you have a 20 percent increased risk of dying from heart disease.)

5. Death from lung cancer occurs **10 times** more often in smokers than nonsmokers (and for people who began smoking before age 15, cancer rates are 19 times higher!).

6. Smoking will discolor your teeth, cause receding gums, and make the skin around your mouth wrinkled.

7. The *British Medical Journal* reported that even after smoking a few cigarettes a day for only two years, young smokers appear considerably less healthy than their nonsmoking peers and show evidence of early obstruction of airways, persistent coughing, and shortness of breath with mild exertion.

8. Two of the Marlboro men, David McLean and Wayne McLaren, died of lung cancer.

9. The Lucky Strike ad spokeswoman, Janet Sackman, now breathes through a gauze-covered hole in her neck; her larynx was removed because of throat cancer caused by cigarette smoking.

10. Quoted in *The Wall Street Journal*, July 25, 1989: the former Winston Man said, "What I did for the past seven years is wrong. I glamorized something that kills you." He became aware of the risks involved in smoking when he had a stroke at age 34!

11. Smoking is even bad for the environment! It is estimated that up to 25 percent of all timber burned throughout the world is used curing tobacco.

12. Chewing tobacco is also bad for you. It not only discolors teeth and damages the gums, but also causes mouth and throat cancers.

A smoker's chance of surviving the use of tobacco is very low.

⇨ **Five out of 10 smokers die of smoking-related disease (50%).**

⇨ **Two out of 10 smokers will be diagnosed as having some type of cancer (20%).**

⇨ **Ten out of 10 long-term smokers develop emphysema (100%).**

⇨ **Nine out of 10 smokers diagnosed with lung cancer die of lung cancer (90%).**

⇨ **Two out of 10 smokers are diagnosed with heart disease (20%).**

⇨ **One out of 10 smokers will be disabled (10%).**

Source: Vibrant Life, 9-93, Special Issue, "How to Stop Smoking"

In some areas cigars have become the latest craze. I call it crazy because a cigar is still just a nicotine delivery system. Cancer death rates for cigar smokers are **34 percent** higher than for nonsmokers! And **99%** of cigar smokers have atypical cells in their voice boxes, which is the first step toward cancer. The smoke from one cigar equals the smoke of three cigarettes, so cigar smokers are poisoning the rest of us with their second-hand smoke.

This equation is simple and brutal:

SMOKING = SLOW SUICIDE

According to former U.S. Surgeon General C. Everett Koop, the tobacco industry spends over $4 billion each year on advertising. That figures out to **over $10 million a day** spent on slick ads with glamorous, athletic people, to try to lure you and me to use this miserable product. Now I ask you, if a product is good, doesn't it sell itself—by just a little advertising and mainly by word of mouth? Why does the tobacco industry have to spend so much money on advertising? Because they need 4000 replacement smokers every day to replace the ones who quit or die that day!

The tobacco industry is moving its markets to Third World countries where there is little information about the harm of the product. Whenever I travel to countries like Malaysia and Africa, I find large numbers of people smoking, and when I discuss this problem with them, they are always surprised—totally unaware that there is any danger in smoking! They look at me like I'm crazy when I say it can cause heart disease and cancer. That's the way it was in the United States in the 1950s, when cigarettes were actually advertised as good for your health!

If you smoke or use smokeless tobacco, *quit now* before the addiction becomes stronger. If you are a friend or relative of someone who smokes, encourage that person to quit. My husband and I even took a friend on vacation with us for a week, threw away his cigarettes, and told him that we were going to have so much fun that he wouldn't have time to smoke. We kept him in the ocean snorkeling most of the time, which is not conducive to smoking! He was grumpy (the body craves the nicotine and feels bad without it), but managed to quit.

There are a number of PPR responses that will help you turn down an offer of tobacco.

- **Simply Say No.** Tell your friend, "Thanks but no thanks."

- **Make An Excuse.** Use a true excuse (as always), such as "I'm in athletics and trying to stay in good shape," or "I can't stand the smell of cigarette smoke."

- **Act Shocked.** For example, "I can't believe you smoke! Let me tell you about some relatives I've lost because of their smoking habit."

- **Flattery.** Say to your friend, "I think so much of you. You've got to quit. Tell me how I can help." You can combine this form of flattery (actually, true concern) with other responses. It's a nice touch and lets your friend know you care.

- **Make a Joke.** There are many lines you can select from! For example:

  "No thanks. I'm not into body pollution."

  "I don't want any cancer sticks today."

  "Don't you know the *real* reason why dinosaurs became extinct? They smoked!"

  "Not my brand. I only smoke Lou Llamas."

  "I'm not into coffin nails today."

  "Are you asking me if I mind being given cancer?!"

I know no one who has used tobacco for a while who doesn't wish that he or she had never smoked that first cigarette or touched that first wad of smokeless tobacco. Older users of tobacco will themselves tell you what an awful habit it is. We can learn a lot from them.

USE OF ALCOHOL

Many people don't think of alcohol as a drug, but it is. It's a Class II narcotic and in the same category as tranquilizers and barbituates, drugs that slow down the central nervous system (which includes the brain). Think of your central nervous system as the body's "command headquarters" and you'll understand how much damage alcohol can do to a body. You may wonder why alcohol is legal for adults if it is a drug. The truth is, alcohol has been around for thousands of years—long before the medical world had much knowledge about it. If alcohol were to be discovered today, it would never be made legal. But it is so widely accepted that to try to outlaw it would be almost impossible.

The active ingredient in alcohol is a chemical called ethyl alcohol. If you remove the water from ethyl alcohol, you get ether, the anesthetic use to put the brain to sleep during surgery. When a person drinks, the liver filters alcohol from the blood steam and eliminates it from the body. The liver can filter about one ounce of alcohol per hour. If someone drinks more than an ounce per hour, the person becomes intoxicated, or drunk. Notice the word *toxic* is part of *intoxication*. Toxic means poisonous! When you are experiencing any of the effects of alcohol, such as slurred speech, slower reaction times, vomiting, slowed-down heartbeat, and dizziness, you are having symptoms of poisoning! And if alcohol is taken into the body at too fast a rate, the brain basically "goes to sleep" and forgets to tell the heart to beat and your body to breathe. So you die—it's called acute alcoholic poisoning.

The news is full of tragedies related to alcohol use. Recently in my community, an 18-year-old who was driving home from work was hit by a young drinking driver and killed. And then there was the popular cheerleader who, as a result of her boyfriend's crash, was thrown out of his sports car and died on the road. Her boyfriend had been seen drinking earlier at the football game. And then there were the two girls who, cruising around late one night, paid dearly for their poor decision making. The girl driving pulled out in front of a police car that was traveling at high speed to help an officer needing assistance. She apparently didn't see his car. Both girls were killed. The girl driving was found to be legally intoxicated. Another incident took place after the senior prom. Some local students checked into a hotel to celebrate. Two guys, who had been drinking, got into a scuffle in the hotel room and begin fighting. One threw the other into a plate-glass window, which broke. That young graduate fell to his death. I could go on . . . and on . . . and on.

Alcohol has also touched the lives of people who are close friends of mine. One friend, when she was a college student, attended a rowdy fraternity party where most people were drinking. She was hit in the face by a flying beer bottle and will have a scar for life. Another friend's car was hit when a drunk driver ran a red light. Her car was totaled and she suffered numerous broken bones. My former boss was hit by a car while walking across a street—again by a drinking driver. Once an avid runner, he now has so many leg injuries that he won't ever be able to run again. The boy who lived next to my parents went party-hopping with his girlfriend following their high school graduation. He was a star basketball player and had already been accepted to college on an athletic scholarship. He never made it to college, because he and some buddies chose to drink at the parties and between the parties. Early in the morning, the driver missed a curve in the road and they crashed. Five of the six teens in the car died. And a junior high girl I know was raped at a party after having passed out from drinking. She doesn't know who raped her, how many took part, and so forth.

The fact is:

ALCOHOL IS THE NUMBER ONE KILLER OF TEENAGERS

So many lives are wasted because of someone's desire to ingest a chemical that we *know* alters a person's mind and mood, interferes with good judgment and vision, slows down muscle control and reaction time, and produces the dangerous feeling of having more power or control than usual.

Many teens tell me they drink not only to appear more grown-up but also to feel comfortable—to loosen up—in social situations. Some say alcohol helps them overcome shyness. The truth is, it does loosen you up, but that also means you may do or say things that you would *not* normally say or do if you were thinking clearly! For instance, among teens who have engaged in sexual activity, nearly half admit that they were intoxicated the first time. Many of these individuals would probably have postponed sex until they were more mature, and better prepared for it, had they not been drinking.

Alcohol gives us a fake sense of having fun, appearing sophisticated, and being a good communicator. Where do we get these false images? From the alcohol ads and from movies. They aren't presenting reality. Just ask one of the 6.6 million children under age 18 who live with an alcoholic mother or father.

If you've ever been the only sober person at a social event, then you know how superficial the conversation is when everyone's drinking. There's *no real conversation!* The topics aren't interesting, and even if they were, no one stays on a topic long enough for some in-depth discussion to develop. Plus, people laugh excessively at things that, if they were sober, wouldn't even make them crack a smile. So, although alcohol may make people talkative, what they say isn't worth much. We must learn how to open up and talk to others without using alcohol. We all can do it, and in the process, what we talk about may actually be interesting. When I was single and dating, I used to spend a few minutes before the date thinking of some interesting things to talk about in case the conversation slowed down. I never went on a date without at least five subjects to bring up. I was frequently told by my dates that I was a great conversationalist—they didn't know that I planned it that way!

Because your body is still growing, the negative effects of alcohol can hit you much faster than it would an adult body. Another danger is that alcohol exaggerates the normal depressions and embarrassments that we all have. Alcohol has been linked to teen suicides, which are at an all-time high. It doesn't help us feel too good about ourselves. So many of us seem to be looking for happiness in all the wrong places.

Think of the specific kind of food you *really* hate—the one that will make you gag if you try to eat it. For me, that's asparagus. I *hate* the taste of it; it's gross and makes me sick to my stomach! After the first time I tried it, I never willingly tried it again (on a few occasions, asparagus was hidden in food I was eating, and it made me sick again when I tasted it!). I bet that, like me, you have avoided the food that you dislike the most and have refused to try it a second time.

Now, if you've tasted alcohol, think of the first time you tried it. What did you think about it?

When I ask people that question, most of them reply, "I hated it," or "It was gross" or "yuck" or "horrible." I then ask if they ever tried alcohol again, and many say "yes." Why would they try it again if they disliked the taste so much? We don't try a food we hate a second time. Why do we ever try alcohol again, knowing that we don't like it? One reason and one reason only: peer pressure. Our friends are drinking. Or someone tells us that it's cool. Or we think it'll make us look grown-up. **Don't fall for this way of thinking! Nothing that you drink will make you cool! You are what's cool—your real self! Not the fake person that alcohol causes you to be.**

A very few people have told me that they liked alcohol the first time they tried it. When I ask what they were drinking, they usually answer that it was a wine cooler. The alcohol industry knows that to attract young drinkers, especially females, they need a sweet taste; so they add lots of fruit flavor and sugar to the liquor so that you can't taste the alcohol. Isn't that nice of them? They take away the bad taste for us because they like us so much—right? Yeah, sure. What they like is our money!

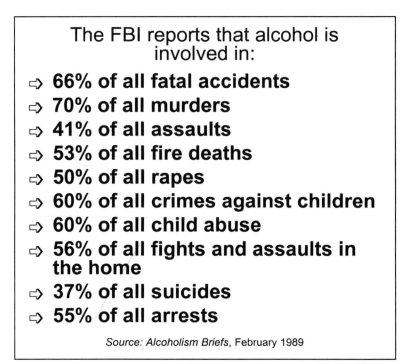

The FBI reports that alcohol is involved in:

⇨ **66% of all fatal accidents**
⇨ **70% of all murders**
⇨ **41% of all assaults**
⇨ **53% of all fire deaths**
⇨ **50% of all rapes**
⇨ **60% of all crimes against children**
⇨ **60% of all child abuse**
⇨ **56% of all fights and assaults in the home**
⇨ **37% of all suicides**
⇨ **55% of all arrests**

Source: Alcoholism Briefs, February 1989

Please delay your decision about whether or not to drink alcohol—wait until you've reached age 21, when you'll have had time to study the effects of it and to allow your body to grow healthy and strong. And when making that decision later on, at age 21, keep in mind that people drink primarily because it's the social thing to do. Because everyone else is doing something is no reason to do anything!

I'm an adult who has chosen not to drink alcohol based on the research of its potential harm to the body. I go to nightclubs with friends, to parties, and so forth, but I order a nonalcoholic drink. I occasionally serve nonalcoholic wine with dinner.

I still get peer pressure to drink. One instance happened at a holiday party held at the Grand Kempinski Hotel in Dallas. When my husband and I arrived in the ballroom, the hostess greeted us and offered to get us a drink. My husband ordered a ginger ale and I ordered ice water (I had just finished an all-day workshop, had been talking nonstop, and was parched!). As she left to get our drinks, she said, "Party poopers!" I thought that was rather rude, but I didn't say anything. When she returned with our drinks, this is how the conversation went:

Hostess: "Sharon, don't you drink?"

Sharon: "Yes, I drink. Iced tea, soft drinks, water, orange juice . . ." (She interrupts me.)

Hostess: "No, dear. I mean, don't you drink alcohol?"

Sharon: "No."

Hostess: "Why not?"

Sharon: "An educated decision."

Hostess: "Oh, are you a recovering alcoholic?"

Can you believe it!! How rude and pressuring can you get! I'm an adult—you would think that I could drink water without someone making a big deal out of it. And you would expect that people would not make such assumptions in public. But they do, and we've all got to learn to live with it and live with them.

Why do people want us to do what they want to do? Because it validates *their* actions. People think that if they can get others to do what they are doing, then doing it is O.K. That kind of reasoning is not only faulty, but dangerous.

What happened next at the party is funny. Some other people overheard the conversation between the hostess and me. They began to ask me what I meant by not drinking because of an educated decision. I told them briefly that I was a counselor and that I sometimes speak on the harmful effects of alcohol. They wanted to hear more. I talked and continued to answer their questions. It always amazes me that people drink alcohol, but know so little about it. When the wine steward came around to our table to pour wine, I noticed that everyone declined. Everyone started laughing and said they wanted to get more information on alcohol. Hooray for their logical thinking! Sometimes—not always, but sometimes— when we stand up for ourselves and healthy decisions, others will learn from us.

I recently attended the latest of my high school class reunions. Over the years, I've noticed that class members who drank in high school, and who appeared to drink heavily at the reunions, looked *much* older than the rest of us. At the reunion I learned that one class member— a heavy drinker—had died in a violent accident; another— also a heavy drinker—had committed suicide.

Along with aging your skin, alcohol adds lots of calories to your diet. Beer bellies and "love handles" (flab around your waist) are not attractive! And it doesn't take much beer or other alcohol to put on the pounds.

We've looked at a number of reasons not to drink. Now let's take a look at which PPR responses are helpful when you want to decline alcohol.

- **Simply Say No.** Saying "no thanks" is a good start. If that doesn't work, you can try other PPR responses.

- **Suggest a Better Idea.** ("I've got a great idea. Why don't we go to that new movie that just came out?")

- **Change the Subject.** ("Let's talk about what we want to do this summer. I want a clear head. Should we go to camp, get a job, or what?")

- **Act Shocked.** This is usually an effective response. ("I didn't know you drank! Your parents will kill you if they find out!")

- **Make a Joke.** The following lines can deflect pressure in a funny way:

  "Oh, darling, I only drink the finest champagne." (Should your friend happen to have champagne, then say, "That's not a very good year.")

  "I never drink before I'm drunk." (By the time they scratch their head and figure that one out, you can be on your merry way!)

  "Not my brand."

  "I'd rather hang loose than hangover."

"I don't need booze to loosen up. I just got it together."

"I'm allergic—makes my skin turn purple and I look like Barney."

"If I drank that, I'd probably forget where I parked my brain."

"You want me to barf all over your car? I didn't think so!"

"No booze is good booze."

"I heard alcohol kills brain cells and I don't have any to spare!"

"Nope, all alcohol does for you is make you vegetate, urinate, and regurgitate!"

Having fun without alcohol has all the advantages. So remember, delay your drinking decision until you're an adult, and think carefully even then. And never, ever get in the car with a ***drinking driver***—which means anyone at the wheel who has been, or is, drinking alcohol. Notice that I didn't use the words *drunk driver*. People under the influence of alcohol never realize they're drunk; they say they're O.K. and capable of driving. *You* know better! If a friend of yours has been drinking and plans to drive, take some action if at all possible. *Don't let that person get behind the wheel of a car.* Take away the car keys and get your friend a safe ride home. You may not only save your friend's life, but the lives of others in the car and on the road.

USE OF OTHER DRUGS

Marijuana (also called pot, grass, weed, reefer), LSD, crack cocaine, inhalants, MDMA (also called ecstasy), and so forth are just some of the drugs that you may be offered one day. These are drugs that can make you dull and dumb. Some of them can kill. Shocking but true, the amount of ecstasy needed to get intoxicated is very close to the *toxic* dose. Drugs have ruined, and even taken, the lives of many people. And fame and money make no difference: there are many famous movie stars, athletes, and musicians who would still be alive and entertaining us if it weren't for their drug use. I went to college during the 1960s when drugs were at their peak, and I saw firsthand how they can screw people up. And most drugs on the street now are *much* stronger (and therefore more harmful) than the drugs of the 1960s.

I'm going to focus on marijuana in this section because of the widespread misperception that it's a harmless drug. Some say it's no worse than alcohol. Even if that were true, think back to the harm that alcohol has done to so many. While alcohol stays in the system only 24 hours, marijuana can still be found in the body at least one month after use! In animal studies it has been proven to stay in the body over four months, and it may do so in the human body, too. In other words, it has a longer time to do its damage.

Marijuana comes from the *Cannabis sativa* plant. Marijuana is a mixture of leaves, stems, and the flowering tops of this plant. Marijuana has 421 different chemicals in it. Scientists have studied only about one-fourth of these chemicals, and they've found some troubling ones, especially delta-9-tetrahydrocannabinol (THC). We'll talk more about THC in a minute, but get this: once you light a joint (a marijuana cigarette), those 421 chemicals change into 2000 different chemicals, which will enter the body with every "hit" off that joint!

What else is in the marijuana is anybody's guess. Some time ago, there was a hospital in Louisiana that had a lot of admissions for salmonella poisoning, which is commonly called food poisoning. It can be very dangerous, even life threatening. They asked all of the patients where they had eaten in the past 24 hours, and found that none of the patients had eaten the same food or gone to a common restaurant. This really stumped the doctors, who became increasingly worried since more and more critically ill patients were being admitted with salmonella. Finally, they decided to conduct a survey to see what these ill patients had in common. They had to find the source of this poisonous outbreak.

When the surveys were completed, the only common factor was that all of these people smoked marijuana. Marijuana does a lot of bad stuff to the body, but it's not known for causing food poisoning! So the doctors asked the patients to provide them with some samples of the marijuana they had been smoking. When tests were run on it, they found that dried dung (cow manure) had been mixed in with the pot! The marijuana sellers could make more money if they made the pot go farther by mixing something cheap (or free) in it. In other words, 2 pounds of marijuana plus half a pound of cow manure equals 2 and a half pounds of drug to sell. It gives a whole new meaning to the common remark from pot-smokers, "Man, this is really good s___." Imagine how stupid those patients felt when they found out how they had contracted salmonella!

THC likes fat, so it seeks out the organs in your body with the highest fat content. Those would be the brain, liver, lungs, and reproductive organs.

The brain is a living computer composed of millions of cells. Those cells have "bridges" between them. Scientists call those bridges "synapses." In a healthy brain, the synapses are open and clear so that electrical impulses (which translate to our thought processes) can travel easily from cell to cell. In the brain of a person who uses marijuana, the synapses fill with THC. So thoughts have difficulty reaching the other side and thinking is slowed down. That is why grades drop and athletic ability slows for most people who use marijuana. There is damage to the hypothalamus, which is the memory center of the brain. That's the reason why the slang term for marijuana is **dope**. I heard a famous neuroscientist once say that marijuana makes a bright person dull and a slow person stupid. And I've seen just that with my clients in my counseling practice.

Pot is also harmful to the lungs. Look at what's in it besides the THC: nicotine (this is added to insect repellent to kill bugs), tar (this is used in the asphalt on our roadways), and carbon monoxide (which comes out of the tail pipe of a running car). Really good stuff, huh? Marijuana has more cancer-causing ingredients than regular cigarettes, can cause precancerous lesions in the lungs in as quickly as two to three years, and makes the lungs more susceptible to emphysema and bronchitis. Marijuana smoking also decreases white blood cell production, which makes it harder to fight off infections, meaning that the user will get more colds and flu.

Of particular importance to teens is that marijuana slows the body's development during puberty. In males, the chest and arm muscles won't grow as they should; as a result, male teens will end up having weak-looking bodies. Just look at the rock stars who are known potheads—their faces look like those of grown men, but their bodies resemble those of young teens. Guys who smoke marijuana have a 50 percent decrease in testosterone, the principal male hormone (what makes one a male). Moreover, their sperm may undergo abnormalities, and they may even experience breast enlargement. In females, often the menstrual cycle is disrupted. It's also possible that the ova (the female reproductive cells, or eggs) will undergo some damage. This means that a girl who smokes marijuana may be causing harm to a child she'll have in the future!

In both males and females, emotional problems surface and often worsen. It affects personality, bringing on *amotivational syndrome*, which is best described as not caring about anything—such as school grades, following rules, and so forth. One of my clients was a national horseriding champion and working toward competing in the Olympics. After she began using marijuana, she wouldn't even go to the stables to feed and pet her beloved horse. Her parents ended up selling this valuable animal to someone who would love and care for him. Her lifelong dreams would never be achieved because of her smoking dope.

The final danger of marijuana—besides the expense, the decrease in energy, and the waste of money—is the development of tolerance. Tolerance means that the body has become used to a substance and therefore needs more and more of it in order to be as affected by it. In terms of marijuana use, smokers will need more of the drug as time goes by in order to get as high from it as they did in the beginning. Which means they will either increase their usage (and harm) or start trying other drugs.

You can use any of the 10 PPR responses to turn down drugs, but *in every case* then you must **leave the scene**! Failure to do so could lead to your arrest. You can **return the challenge** ("I'm not interested. Do it by yourself if you have to. I should hope that you know better though.") or **make a joke** before **leaving**—but don't drag your feet. Get away *fast*!

It seems like all the **joking** lines I know for saying no to drugs are *really* stupid. Don't boo me—appreciate my weird sense of humor. Here they are:

"I just popped some M&Ms, can't handle any more
today."

"Is that a low-tar joint? That's the only kind I'll smoke."
(Obviously there is no such thing.)

"I don't smoke grass, just mow it once a week!"
(Did I hear you boo me?)

If the person offering you drugs is a good friend, you
might want to **act shocked** ("We need to have a talk about
this later. Surely you know how harmful that stuff is!"), or
use **flattery** (You're too smart to use dope. I don't want to
see you hurt."). But again, you must then **leave the scene**.

Some people suggest that we should let individuals who
use drugs do so. After all, they say, these individuals aren't
harming anyone but themselves. How wrong! Check out
any maternity ward and you'll see babies born brain-
damaged and already addicted because of their mother's
use of drugs. Go to any elementary school and ask about
the prevalence of learning disabilities in children, many of
them struggling to read and write because of damage
caused by their parents' drug use.

Also consider that many people are robbed or burglar-
ized by drug users who are desperate for money to buy
more drugs. Check out some of the countries where
newspaper reporters and editors have been assassinated
by drug lords because they reported on the harm of drugs.
Notice the increase of violence in countries (including the
United States) where drugs are a serious problem, and the
countless loss of law enforcement officers who are trying
to control this problem.

To close this section, I want to tell you about my friend, Larry Cadena. Larry was a police officer whom I worked with years ago at the Dallas Police Department. He was a good and fair officer and well liked. Some time after I left the department, he asked to be transferred to the Narcotics Division because he was concerned about the local drug problem. He didn't want to see happen to his children what he had seen happen to so many others.

Larry accepted an undercover assignment to try to infiltrate a gang that was selling drugs in east Dallas. Of course, it took a while to get the members of the gang to trust him enough to sell him drugs. Finally, they agreed to sell "their friend," Larry, $5000 worth of cocaine. The plan was for Larry to meet them at a certain location at midnight the following night.

The next night as Larry sat in his car, the drug dealers showed up. What they didn't know was that Larry was an undercover police officer. They didn't know that he had a tiny microphone on him; nor did they know that within a block were two cars full of undercover officers ready to make the arrest after the deal went down.

After a brief conversation, Larry showed them that he had the money for the drugs. Instead of giving him the cocaine, though, one of the drug dealers pulled an automatic rifle from under his trench coat, pointed it at Larry's chest, and pulled the trigger four times. Larry died at the scene.

The other undercover officers came running from their cars, yelling "Police! Put down your weapons!" The gang members shot at the police. The police returned fire. One drug dealer dropped dead in the street. Two others, ages 17 and 19, dropped their weapons. They were all arrested and found guilty of murder. They are currently in the Huntsville, Texas, penitentiary for life sentences.

The end to this true, sad story is that the cocaine they showed Larry that night was not even genuine. They wanted money from him without even giving him the drugs.

I don't care if a dealer is 12 or 40 years old. All dealers are scum. They don't care about you or me or about our health and well-being. And users, well, they're the biggest part of this problem, because if there weren't a demand for the product, it wouldn't be around in the first place. Let's remember the people like Larry who are willing to give their lives for our health and safety. The least we should do is become part of the solution by never using illegal drugs. And, if you want to do more, consider the following:

1. Join a club at your school that has a goal of staying chemical-free—or start one if your school doesn't have one. (Consider reading another of my books for teens, *When to Say Yes! And Make More Friends*, which focuses on the subject of peer helping.)

2. Plan a Red Ribbon Day at your school to gain support of the drug-free way as the way to be!

3. Give "soft-drink parties." Or learn to make "mocktails," not cocktails. For example, pina coladas without the alcohol are fabulous! And don't say no one will come if you don't serve alcohol—some will and some won't. I always have alcohol-free parties and am known for it.

4. Suggest to your language arts teachers that they sponsor a contest on "Why I Choose to Be Drug-Free."

5. Be creative when planning social events at school. There are many things to do that aren't associated with alcohol, such as dances might be. Ideas include having pool parties, Dress Like Your Pet contests, cookouts, skating or rollerblading events, and lock-ins. I know of some students who, as a class, conduct money-making projects beginning in their freshman year and use the funds for a big senior trip, such as a Caribbean cruise or a weekend in New York. Everyone knows there will be no alcohol or other drugs involved. The rule is, if anyone uses these substances during the trip, they will be sent home with no refund.

6. Put up posters or a bulletin board in your school devoted to the harm of drugs and alternative things to do for fun (natural highs as opposed to artificial, chemical ones).

7. Plan a blast for prom night, but heavily promote it as chemical-free. Make little cards that say, "Friends don't let friends use drugs. Have a fun and chemical-free evening." Give them to the florists and tuxedo shops to put in each order.

8.   Encourage your school and other youth groups to bring speakers in for a presentation on being drug-free, managing peer pressure, planning chemical-free parties, and so forth. Or the speaker can work at a retreat with a small group of students, who in turn will work with other students.

9.   Write an article for your school newspaper, or a letter to the editor of your town's newspaper, commending students who remain chemical-free.

10. Encourage your art or drama teacher to assign some kind of study of the media's impact on society's use of drugs. For example, the study could focus on movies or advertisements, and the drug-related messages they send to us.

You can make a difference.

SEX

The main reason why teens become sexually involved is that their partners pressure them into it. In a misguided effort to keep their boyfriend or girlfriend, they launch into the world of sexual experience before they're truly ready for it. The truth is, there's no way to hold on to someone who doesn't share your love. Having sex with that person only causes loss of self-esteem, the feeling of being used, fear of pregnancy, and fear of sexually transmitted diseases (STDs). In fact, many people lose interest in their partner after having sex—often they just wanted to see how far the other one would really go, or they had a bet with someone that they could "score."

We also have the impression that "everyone is doing it." However, approximately 50 percent of graduating seniors have chosen **not** to be sexually active. There are many youth who claim to be sexually active but actually aren't. They're afraid they won't fit in with the "in crowd" if they don't talk about their exploits, too. That's sad. Besides, this is a subject that should be private and discussed only between the involved parties.

The second most common reason why teens have sex with someone is that they think they're in love. And maybe some of them are, but they'll probably be "in love" with quite a few people before they get married some day. If we choose to have sex with every one we think we're in love with, we might develop a history that we'll someday regret.

I didn't get married until I was 31 years old. Looking back, I had a lot of romances that at the time I thought meant love. The guys were cute, nice, friendly, and treated me well, but not one of them was someone I would have ever married. Just because we are attracted to someone and have strong feelings for him or her, it doesn't mean we've a good reason to have sex with that person. It took me a long time to find my husband, and that long time allowed me to mature and know who I really was and what I wanted. As a result, we have a successful, happy marriage. Because we were older when we got married, we didn't have the financial problems that young married couples often face. I already had a house, and my husband owned quite a bit of land; both of us even had our cars paid for!

My theme in this section is going to be **Just Say Wait**. There is a time and a place for everything, including sexual activity. Rely on your parents' values and your own moral upbringing as you think about this issue. Consider delaying your sexual activity until marriage. Marriage has with it a *commitment* by two people to love and honor and support each other forever. It also includes legal obligations to each other in case of death or divorce. It's a statement to society of a couple's intentions and gives stability to the union. (In fact, marriage is "in" again. Many have found that the divorce rate is actually higher among those who lived together prior to marriage!) When we're *truly* committed, marriage is in order and a sexual relationship can begin.

Our society has always been based on the family—whose members should be people we can rely on. However, millions of teenage girls have discovered that they had no loyalty from the fathers of their unborn children. When they told their boyfriends about their pregnancy, they heard some of these classic lines: "It's not mine. See ya!"; "You're not going to have it, are you?"; or "Sure, I'll help you," the father never to be seen again. In some cases, teens do marry after learning about the pregnancy, but teenage marriages are known for problems and ultimately breaking up. The trouble is, there's still so much personal growth to experience! People's personalities, opinions, and thoughts change a great deal in the late teens and early 20s. In many ways, you aren't the "final you" until you're much older.

If you think it's not that easy to get pregnant, think again. Keep in mind that the United States has the highest teen pregnancy rate of any industrialized country. Also consider that it's not fair to you, your partner, your parents, or an unborn child to put yourself in a position to conceive a child when you do not have the resources to fully provide for that child. That means you have your *own* salary, housing, transportation, and education to rear that child to age 18—which will cost a lot of money. To ask your parents to take on the expense of another child is not fair to them, nor is it right for the child to come into this world not having its own family who wants it, loves it, and can support it without the financial help of family or welfare. That may sound hard. But I've spent a career seeing what happens to children who were not wanted or could not be cared for properly. We need to get beyond our selfishness and think a lot about the future—not just what we feel like doing in a moment of passion.

WARNING: SEX CAN BE HAZARDOUS TO YOUR HEALTH

Also consider these facts:

⇨ **Over 3 million teenagers are infected each year with any one of the 20 STDs identified so far.** About 1 out of every 6 sexually active teens has an STD.

⇨ **80% of all people with STDs don't even know they are infected!**

⇨ **The most common STD, chlamydia, can cause so much damage to the fallopian tubes that a woman could be childless for life.**

⇨ **Other STDs have no known cure.** Thirty-one million Americans have genital herpes, which causes painful blisters. There is also no cure if you get human papilloma virus (HPV), which causes genital warts. There are 24 million cases of HPV.

⇨ **Women who have had multiple sex partners run a much higher risk of getting cervical cancer.**

⇨ **Over one million teens become pregnant each year.** Young girls have more problems during pregnancy because their bodies are still growing and not ready for motherhood. Babies born to young mothers suffer more health problems also.

⇨ **There is no known cure for AIDS.** You will die if you get it. The *American Medical News* reported that *heterosexual* transmission of HIV (the virus that develops into AIDS) has increased 44% since 1989.

There is really no such thing as safe sex. You may have heard that it's safe if you use a latex condom with non-oxynol 9 as a lubricant. It can help, but it's not foolproof. You can still get genital herpes and genital warts *even* using a condom. And condoms can break. If that happens and your partner has AIDS, you die. Sexual abstinence is the only safe approach to sex—until you are married to an uninfected, faithful partner.

Sex *can* wait until you're married. Even if you've already had sex, you can still decide to not do so again until marriage (some people call it secondary virginity). So you think you're in love now, but you've decided not to have sex. What do you do? Read on.

Ways to Show Love Without Having Sex

Hugging and kissing obviously express our affection, but they're not the only ways to show your love for a person. Try some of the approaches below!

❤ giving compliments ❤ picking him up from work ❤ letting her little brother or sister go on a date with you once ❤ writing him a love letter ❤ buying a small gift that reminds you of her ❤ picking out a special video that you know he will like ❤ showing up to watch his team play ❤ not calling her when you know she's tired ❤ dedicating a song on the radio to him ❤ saying only nice things about her to others ❤ cooking a dinner together ❤ planning ahead a fun activity rather than saying "I don't care what we do" ❤ holding hands ❤ doing homework together ❤ walking in the park together ❤ drawing him a picture or writing her a poem ❤ surprising him with a picnic that you prepared ❤ selecting your song ❤ sending (or picking) her one perfect rose of her favorite color ❤ jogging together ❤ winking at each other across a crowded room ❤ baking his favorite cookies or giving her candy ❤ carrying her school books ❤ washing his car ❤ having a special photograph made of you as a gift ❤ giving him a laugh by clipping a funny cartoon from the paper ❤ gazing into each other's eyes ❤ playing her favorite video game even though it bores you ❤ respecting one another ❤ sharing your future dreams ❤ sending him a funny card for no reason ❤ being the best listener in the whole world ❤ just being there ❤

Notice from that list what love is. It's mutual caring and respect.

Love is never violent.

Too many young women confuse their boyfriend's jealousy with love. A person never slaps, hits, kicks, or shoves a person he or she loves. A 14-year-old girl whom I recently worked with had bruises on her from her boyfriend. She felt that he really loved her because he slapped her around to make her "do right." What he was really doing was attempting to control her. He belonged to a gang and used drugs and was out of control. He had no skills at controlling his temper and took this out on her. Stay clear immediately and forever from anyone who physically hurts you! This is *not* love. It's abuse! If you've seen this violence in your own home, between your parents, then it can be confusing to know what love really is. It's really about kindness.

Love is not possessive.

If someone really cares about you, then you don't have to check up on that person or demand that he or she see no one else. If a person really loves you, then he or she won't want to date others. It will come naturally. A person who loves you will let you see other friends, too, and accept that as part of your world. Love never stalks. It's really about trust.

Love is not demanding.

If someone really cares about you, then he or she will understand when you want to delay sexual activity and will wait for you. Love is not in a hurry, because it will always be there. It's really about respect.

LOVE IS . . .
❤ KINDNESS
❤ TRUST
❤ AND RESPECT

There are a lot of lines that you may hear from boyfriends or girlfriends to encourage you to become sexually involved with them. The lines often are intended to break down your resistance and sometimes even to make you feel inferior. Be aware that nowadays, it's not just guys who cause the problem; girls also come on to guys sometimes. They think they can hold on to guys with sex, or they want to brag to their friends, or they lack dating skills such as planning activities and communicating.

Here are some of the more common come-on lines and suggested replies:

"If you really loved me, you'd do this with me."

- **"If you really loved me, you'd quit pressuring me to do something I'm not ready for."** *(Return the Challenge)*

- **"Are you asking me to marry you?"** *(Make a Joke)*

- **"Oh, so you want to be a daddy (or mommy)?"** *(Act Shocked)*

"You don't understand. It really hurts me to not go any further."

- **"I'm sorry. I've heard a cold shower might help."** *(Suggest a Better Idea)*

- **"Maybe we should double date for a while, so we both can cool down."** *(Suggest a Better Idea)*

- **"I really like you a lot, but I just want to be friends."** *(Flattery* and *Make an Excuse)*

"You're beautiful and sexy. You really turn me on."

- **"Thank you and so are you, but I'm not going any further. My belief is that it's wrong before marriage."** *(Flattery* and *Make an Excuse)*

- **"I sound like electricity—and I have a power outage."** *(Make a Joke)*

- **"I just want you to hold me. Nothing more."** *(Suggest a Better Idea* and *Simply Say No)*

"Why won't you do it with me? Are you frigid?"

- **"Your rude comments are what's cold! I want to go home if you intend to put me down further."** *(Act Shocked* and *Suggest a Better Idea)*

- **"That's really a rude thing to say. If you really cared about me, you wouldn't say such things."** *(Act Shocked* and *Return the Challenge)*

- **"Speaking of frigid, it's cold here. I've got a great idea. Let's go to my house and I'll make us some hot chocolate and we can watch a late movie."** *(Ignore the Peer* and *Suggest a Better Idea)*

"You're a real tease. I thought you wanted to. Don't be scared."

- **"If I were going to have sex with someone, it would be with you. I like you a whole lot, but I'm waiting until I get married."** *(Flattery* and *Make an Excuse)*

- **"Excuse me, but having a baby does scare me. And it should scare you, too!"** *(Act Shocked)*

- **"I only tease you because I like you. I didn't mean to give you the wrong impression. Do you like people teasing you? Let me tell you about the time I teased my brother and it caused him to fall down and he broke his arm!"** *(Flattery* and *Change the Subject)*

And never fall for these losing lines:

"You can't get pregnant the first time." (A LIE!)

"If I had AIDS, you could tell." (WRONG!)

"I won't give you any STDs." (If they've had sex with anyone else, it's likely they WILL!)

"I'll marry you if you get pregnant." (Yeah, sure! Besides, who wants to start off a marriage fat for nine months, then not be able to go anywhere because you have a baby and not much money. It's a great way to begin a divorce.)

"No one will find out." (How true, since nothing is going to happen!)

Remember that you don't even have to give someone a reason for not having sex with him or her! It's your decision! Just wait! Ninety-nine percent of the sexually active teens whom I've talked to wished they had waited. They say getting involved in this way is not worth it emotionally. And remember that condoms may provide safer sex from some, but not all, STDs. Moreover, if they fail, they cannot protect you from a broken heart, shattered dreams, and maybe even your death.

VIOLENCE

Violence comes in many forms. Obvious forms of violence include gang activity, carrying weapons to school, and date rape. But so are fighting, cursing in public, hitting your date, gesturing hatefully to other drivers, shoving people to get through a crowd, speeding while driving, teaching your dog to be mean, and even name calling! Small acts of violence can easily escalate into the larger acts of violence by which people can get seriously hurt or killed.

Today's news reported the death of a 20-year-old woman who was thrown from her pickup which flipped over after being clipped by a car driven by a 17-year-old boy. The woman was six and a half months pregnant and the baby was delivered at the hospital two hours before his mother was pronounced dead. The premature baby boy died three days later. Police said the boy was driving 80 to 100 mph when he clipped the rear bumper of the woman's car. The boy said he was chasing a car full of girls who were smiling and waving at him.

Although this tragedy was not intentional, to get behind the wheel of a 2,500 pound vehicle and drive at such speed became a senseless act of violence killing two people and ruining the lives of many.

Do we ever encourage violence? I think so. We pay good money to view movies with awfully violent material, making Hollywood think that's what we want the most. When two people get into an argument in the school hallway, we often say, "Hit him!" rather than trying to break it up. Young women often encourage jealousy between two rival boyfriends and think that it's cool if they fight over her. We are lonely for a close family, and some of us seek it in gangs rather than in groups at a recreation facility, at a religious youth group, or at school. We often talk "trash" in public and see just how far we can go. We encourage others to get even rather than work out people problems.

We need to decide what kind of society we want to live in. If we want to have a sane, peaceful place in which to live, then peace must begin with each of us. Sometimes it just takes common sense.

For example, one day I was standing in a school hallway, taking a short break between my presentations. Two girls were walking down the hall on the "wrong" side and bumped into two other girls rounding the corner. One of the girls said, "Get out of my face!" The other girl said, "I'm not in your face. But I would if I wanted to be!" I was saddened by the fact that no one seemed to have any common sense. It was an accident, for goodness sakes. All it called for was a laugh and a quick, "Excuse me." We seem to have lost the art of being polite to one another.

In observing people's actions, I sometimes see hatred towards others because of a difference in race, religion, or gender. We all seem to think that whatever we are is superior to anything different. Can't we appreciate our differences? None of us is better than the other. Nor worse. We're all just different. And, even if we can't always understand others' differences, can't we just respect them? Everyone doesn't have to be our best friend, but we are all capable of being kind to others.

When you're mad at someone, try talking it out. Here are some suggestions that might help:

1. Tell the other person that you'd like to solve the differences between the two of you. Ask the person if there's a time when you can talk to him or her alone. Don't include friends in the discussion, as they complicate the process. The only time they're useful to the discussion is when you have peer mediators at your school. (If you have peer mediators, feel free to ask them for any help you might need; if you don't have them, consider asking your school counselor for help.)

2. Set a time and place.

3. When you begin the conversation, set ground rules such as no name calling, no interrupting, and no walking away mad.

4. Take turns expressing why you're upset. Talk as long as necessary to get it all out.

5. After getting all the opinions out, both of you need to suggest ways to solve the problem. Agree on the best solution(s) and follow through!

This technique can be used when you're mad at your best friend or even your worst enemy. The key is that you give each other time to express feelings and both really listen to one another. You may have to do this several times when things are really serious.

It's not always terribly easy. But the alternatives—staying mad, fuming, or fighting—are more difficult.

Peace can and should begin with each of us. Let's make a commitment to begin the process now. That process includes politeness; showing respect; not cursing publicly; laughing more; being friendlier; learning to talk through, rather than fighting about, problems; avoiding gangs; being kind . . . the list goes on. Add to it whatever you think is needed.

6.

SUMMARY:

THEY CHOOSE,

YOU LOSE

I hope this book has helped you examine your life and where you're going with it. You can be anything that you want to be as long as you don't take a wrong turn and endanger your future. And even if you feel that you've taken a wrong turn, just remember that "tomorrow is the first day of the rest of your life." Begin right now to be the best you can be! All research shows that the most successful people are those who work hard toward their goals—not the brightest or the best-looking, but those who are willing to set their sights high.

How to Say No and Keep Your Friends is simply about doing your own thinking. It's about doing what is *right*. About being proud of who you are and being independent. Being independent doesn't mean that you do things to shock people, but that you know what kind of person you want to be (a decent one) and where you're going (a positive direction toward your future). It's nice to know that you can make good decisions and have lots of friends. With the skill of **Peer Pressure Reversal**, you can be a winner. Use it the rest of your life!

Be courageous and do what's right.

I wish you life's best. Peace.

Consider bringing Sharon Scott to your school or youth group to speak on **Peer Pressure Reversal** (or one of her many other dynamic topics). For information, contact her at:

Sharon Scott's LifeSkills "For Positive Living"
P.O. Box 6
Weston, TX 75097-0006

For information on teaching transparencies for this book or to find out more about Sharon's seven other books, including **Peer Pressure Reversal: An Adult Guide to Developing a Responsible Child**, 2nd Edition (which is the adult companion guide to this book), contact:

HRD Press
22 Amherst Rd.
Amherst, MA 01002
1-800-822-2801 (U.S. and Canada)
413-253-3488 (outside U.S.)
413-253-3490 (fax)

ABOUT THE AUTHOR

Sharon Scott is an experienced family therapist in private practice, author of eight books, international lecturer, native Texan, and currently "mother" to four dogs and two cats. She has taught her Peer Pressure Reversal skills to over one million teens and adults in 41 states and 5 foreign countries.

Before opening her own business, Sharon worked for the Dallas Police Department for seven years serving as Director of the nationally recognized First Offender Program. She also spent four years as a social worker for the Dallas County Department of Human Services.

Sharon has received numerous awards for her efforts, including twice being honored with the "Professional Writing Award" by the Texas Counseling Association and the "Heart of America Award" for her efforts in keeping kids off drugs. She appeared on a nationally aired TV special, *Pressure Points*, with Kirk Cameron and has been interviewed by CNN, *20/20*, *Newsweek*, *Good Morning Australia*, *Teen Magazine*, and many other news and entertainment sources.

Her hobbies include snow skiing, snorkeling, and traveling. She loves nature and her favorite trips have been two photography safaris to Africa and dog mushing in Canada.

OTHER BOOKS BY SHARON SCOTT

Sharon Scott's books are excellent resources for educators, youth leaders, concerned parents, teens, and children. The following titles are now available:

Peer Pressure Reversal,
Second Edition
(for adults)

$14.95 / paperback / 208 pages
Order Code...PPR2

Positive Peer Groups
(for adults)

$9.95 / paperback / 96 pages
Order Code...PPG

When to Say Yes! And Make
More Friends
(grades 5–12)

$7.95 / paperback / 120 pages
Order Code...WTSY

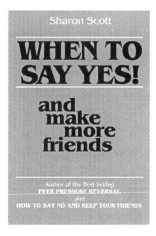

The Nicholas the Cocker Spaniel Series:

Too Smart for Trouble (grades K–4)

(Also available in Spanish from the author)

$7.95 / paperback / 112 pages / Order Code...TST
Set of 11 Teaching Transparencies / $49.95
Order Code...TSTT

Not Better...Not Worse...Just Different (grades K–5)

$7.95 / paperback / 118 pages / Order Code...NBNWD
Set of 16 Teaching Transparencies / $49.95
Order Code...NBNWT

Too Cool for Drugs (grades 1–5)

(Also available in Spanish from the author)

$8.95 / paperback / 120 pages / Order Code...TCD
Set of 17 Teaching Transparencies / $49.95
Order Code...TCDT

Life's Not Always Fair (grades 1–5)

$11.95 / paperback / 124 pages / Order Code...LNAF
Set of 17 Teaching Transparencies / $49.95
Order Code...LNAFT

Also available:

- Nicholas the Cocker Spaniel (14 inch full body hand puppet)
- Teen video (Available from the author)

For ordering information contact:

HRD Press
22 Amherst Road
Amherst, MA 01002

800-822-2801 (U.S. and Canada)
413-253-3488 (all other countries)
Fax: 413-253-3490
http://www.hrdpress.com (Internet)

Discounts given on quantity and prepaid orders.